Thomas E. Waggaman

Catalogue of a Collection of Paintings by European and American Artists,

and of Chinese, Cochin-Chinese, Korean and Japanese Keramics

Thomas E. Waggaman

Catalogue of a Collection of Paintings by European and American Artists,
and of Chinese, Cochin-Chinese, Korean and Japanese Keramics

ISBN/EAN: 9783337240974

Printed in Europe, USA, Canada, Australia, Japan

Cover: Foto ©Thomas Meinert / pixelio.de

More available books at **www.hansebooks.com**

CATALOGUE

OF

A Collection of Paintings

BY

EUROPEAN AND AMERICAN ARTISTS,

AND OF

Chinese, Cochin-Chinese, Korean and Japanese Keramics, &c.

THE PROPERTY OF

THOMAS E. WAGGAMAN,

WITH INTRODUCTION, NOTES AND DESCRIPTIONS BY

EDWARD GREEY,

AUTHOR OF

"The Golden Lotus," "A Captive of Love," "Young Americans in Japan," "The Wonderful City of Tokyo," "The Bear Worshippers of Yezo," &c.

1888.

Paintings.

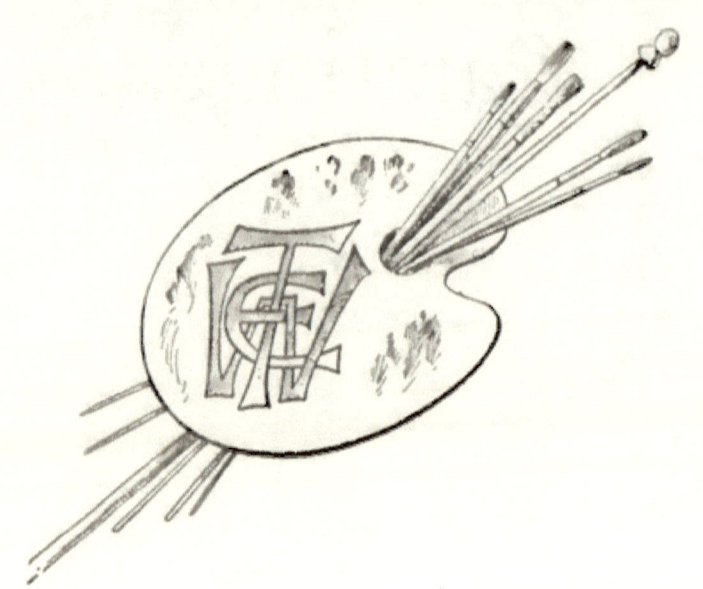

ARTISTS.

No.		Page.
48.	Antigna, J. P. A.	16
46.	Bertrand, J.	16
5.	Boughton, G. H.	7
8.	Bouguereau, W. A.	8
31.	Braith, A.	13
20.	Bridgman, F.	10
11.	Brooke, R. N.	9
21.	Brown, J. G.	11
30.	Brown, J. Lewis	12
74.	Chase, H.	21
58.	Chelminski, J.	18
28.	Chirici, G.	12
54, 77.	Corot, J. B. C.	17, 22
37, 52.	Daubigny, C. F.	14, 17
50.	Daubigny, K P.	16
19.	De Haas, F. H.	10
39.	De Jonghe, G.	14
69.	De La Mar, I.	20
66, 72.	De Neuville, A. M.	20, 21
32.	Decamps, A. G.	13
35.	Delpy, H. C.	14
47.	Deschamps, L.	16
22, 81.	Detaille, E.	11, 23
36, 65.	Diaz, N. V.	14, 19
40.	Dupré, Jules	14
68.	Egusquiza, R.	20
3.	Fromentin, Eugene	7
80.	Galofré, B.	22
64.	Gonzales, J. A.	19

No.		Page
29.	Hagborg, A.	12
53.	Hamon, J. L.	17
2.	Haquette, G.	7
42, 60.	Harpignies, H.	15, 18
14.	Henner, Jean J.	9
27.	Holberg, F.	12
76.	Holmes, W. H.	22
23.	Humborg, A.	11
63.	Inness, G.	19
9, 18.	Jacque, C. E.	8, 10
59, 61.	Jacquet, J. G.	18, 19
79.	Jones, H. Bolton	22
1.	Kaemmerer, F. H.	7
49.	Knight, D. R.	16
6, 25.	Lambinet, E.	8, 11
13.	Leloir, L.	9
78.	Lhermitte, L.	22
44.	Makovski, C.	15
4.	Merle, H.	7
41, 57.	Miralles, F.	15, 18
51.	Moreau, A.	17
62.	Peskoff,	19
70.	Quartley, A.	20
35.	Rousseau, Th.	13
55.	Roybet, Ferdinand	17
7.	Schreyer, A.	8
56.	Schutze, W.	18
34.	Siebert, E.	13
17.	Stevens, Alfred	10
26.	Thédy, M.	12
15, 67.	Toulmouche, A.	9, 20
12, 45.	Troyon, C.	9, 15
16.	Turner, J. W. M.	10
33.	Valentini, V.	13
24.	Unknown,	11
10.	Van Schaick, S.	8
73.	Vibert, J. G.	21
71.	Villegas, Josef	21
43.	Weyl, Max	15
75.	Ziem, F. F. G. P.	21

PAINTINGS.

F. H. KAEMMERER, - - Brussels
    Medal, Paris Salon, 1874.

1   Waiting.

ANTON MAUVE (Deceased),   -   -   Holland
    Pupil of M. P. F. van Os
    Third Medal, Paris, 1887.
    Died, Feb. 1888.

2   Moutons Sortent De La Foret.
           No. 1637. Paris Salon, 1887.

EUGENE FROMENTIN (Deceased),   -   -   -   Paris
    Medals, Paris Salon, 1849-'57-'59.
    Medal, Paris Exposition, 1867.
    Cross of Legion of Honor, 1859.
    Officer Legion of Honor, 1869.

3   Arabs en **Voyage.**

HUGUES MERLE (Deceased),   -   -   -   Paris
    Medals, Paris Salon, 1861-'63.
    Cross of Legion of Honor, 1866.

4   The **Good Sister.**

G. H. BOUGHTON,   -   -   -   -   -   -   London
    N. A. and A. R. A.

5   Winter.

E. LAMBINET (Deceased), - - - - Paris
    Medals, Paris Salon, 1843-'53-'57.
    Cross of Legion of Honor, 1867.

6   The Pasture by the Sea

ADOLPHE SCHREYER, - - - Paris
    Medal, Brussels Exposition, 1863.
    Medals, Paris Salon, 1864-'65.
    Medal, Paris Exposition, 1867.
    Medal, Vienna Exposition, 1874.

7   Wallachian Team at a Ford.

WILLIAM ADOLPHE BOUGUEREAU, - - Paris
    Medals, Exposition Universelle.
    Created Knight of the order of
    Leopold, Grand Medal of Honor
    at Paris, 1883, &c.

8   Going to the Well.

CHARLES EMILE JACQUE, - Paris
    Medals, Paris Salon, 1861-'63-'64.
    Medal, Paris Exposition, 1867.
    Cross of Legion of Honor, 1867.

9   Homeward Bound.

S. VAN SCHAICK, - - - - Brussels

10   The Convalescent.

R. N. BROOKE,   Washington

11   A Quiet Corner.

CONSTANTINE TROYON (Deceased),   Paris
        Medals, Paris Salon, 1838-'40-'46-'48.
        Medal, Paris Exposition, 1855.
        Cross of Legion of Honor, 1849.

12   Cattle at Rest.

LOUIS LELOIR (Deceased),   Paris
        Medals, Paris Salon, 1864-'68-'70.
        Medal, Paris Exposition, 1878.
        Cross of Legion of Honor, 1876.

13   The Martyr.

JEAN JACQUES HENNER,   Paris
        Medals, 1863-'65-'66.
        Legion of Honor, 1873.

14   A Head.

M. RICO,   Paris
        Medal and Legion of Honor, 1878.

15   Canal San Trovaso, Venice.

J. W. M. TURNER (Deceased),   ·   ·   ·   ·   London

16   New Weir on the Wye.

ALFRED STEVENS,   ·   ·   ·   ·   Brussels and Paris

     Medals, Paris Salon, 1853–'55.
     Medals, Paris Expositions, 1867–'78.
     Commander Legion of Honor, 1878.
     Officer Order of Leopold.
     Commander Order of St. Michael of Bavaria.
     Commander Order of Ferdinand of Austria.

17   By the Shore.

C. E. JACQUE,   ·   ·   ·   Paris

     Medals, Paris Salon, 1861–'63–'64.
     Medal, Paris Exposition, 1867.
     Cross of Legion of Honor, 1867.

18   Chickens.

F. H. DE HAAS, N. A.,   ·   ·   ·   New York

19   Moonrise and Sunset.

F. BRIDGMAN,   ·   ·   ·   Paris

     Medal, Paris Salon, 1877.
     Medal, Paris Exposition, 1878.
     Cross of Legion of Honor, 1878.

20   An Oriental Head.

J. G. BROWN, N. A., New York
21 Dull Times.

EDOUARD DETAILLE, Paris
    Medals, Paris Salon, 1869-'70-'72.
    Cross of Legion of Honor, 1873.
    Officer Legion of Honor, 1881.
22 An Equestrian Study.

A. HUMBORG, Munich
    Medals at Munich and Berlin.
23 Among the Casks.

UNKNOWN.
24 The Progress of Christianity.
    (Resembles Guilio Romano.)

E. LAMBINET, Paris
    Medals, Paris Salon, 1843-'53-'57.
    Cross of Legion of Honor, 1867.
25 On the Upper Seine.

M. THÉDY, — Munich
26   A Musical Enthusiast.

F. HOLBERG, — Munich
27   In the Choir—Santa Maria
            Novella—Florence.

GAETANA CHIRICI, — Rome
28   Warming Dolly's Hands.

AUGUSTE HAGBORG, — Paris
   Pupil of Palmaroli.
   Medal, Paris Salon, 1879.
29   The Fisherman's Departure.

J. LEWIS BROWN, — Paris
   Medals, Paris Salon, 1865-'66-'67.
   Cross of Legion of Honor, 1870.
30   Dull Times.

ANTON BRAITH,   Munich

      Medals, Munich, 1869-'76.
      Medals, Vienna, 1873; Dusseldorf, 1880.

31   **Calves.**

ALEXANDRE GABRIEL DECAMPS (Deceased),   Paris

      Pupil of Abel de Pujol, Medals, 1831-'39.
      Legion of Honor, 1839, died, 1860.

32   **A Halt.**

V. VALENTINI, ...   Rome

33   **Head of a Peasant Woman.**

E. SIEBERT,   .   .   .   - New York

34   **A Cavalier.**

THEODORE ROUSSEAU (Deceased),   .   -   .   -   Paris

      Medals, Paris Salon, 1834-'47-'55.
      Grand Medal of Honor, Paris Exposition, 1867.
      Cross of Legion of Honor, 1852. Died, 1867.

35   **A Fisherman's Hut.**

N. V. DIAZ (Deceased),　　　　　　　　　　　　　　　Paris
  Medals, Paris Salon, 1844-'46-'48.
  Cross of Legion of Honor, 1851.

36　　　　　　　Cupids at Play.

C. F. DAUBIGNY (Deceased),　·　　·　　　　　　Paris
  Medals, Paris Salon, 1843-'53-57.
  Medals, Paris Expositions, 1855-'67.
  Cross of Legion of Honor, 1859.
  Officer Legion of Honor, 1869.

37　　　　　Early Morning—A Study.

H. C. DELPY,　·　·　　·　　　　·　　　Paris
  Pupil of C. F. Daubigny.

38　　　　　A Normandy Village.

G. DE JONGHE,　·　　　·　　　　　　Brussels
  Medal, Paris Salon, 1863.
  Knight of the Order of Leopold.
  Order of the Rose of Brazil.

39　　　　　　A Lady at Home.

JULES DUPRÉ,　·　　·　·　·　·　　·　Paris
  Medal, Paris Salon, 1833.
  Medal, Paris Exposition, 1867.
  Cross of the Legion of Honor, 1849.
  Officer Legion of Honor, 1870.

40　　　　　A Summer Landscape.

F. MIRALLES,   Paris
    Pupil of Madrazo.

41   Shall I or shall I not.

HENRI HARPIGNIES,   Paris
    Medals, Paris Salon, 1866-'68-'69.
    Cross of Legion of Honor, 1875.

42   Twilight.

MAX WEYL,   Washington, D. C

43   Twilight.

C. MAKOVSKI,   St. Petersburg

44   A Head.

CONSTANTINE TROYON (Deceased),   Paris
    Medals, 1840-'46-'48-'55.
    Legion of Honor, 1840.

45   The Return to the Farm.

J. BERTRAND, · · · Paris
>Medals, Paris Salon, 1861-'63-'69.
>Medal, Paris Exposition, 1878.
>Cross of Legion of Honor, 1878.

46   Marguerite.

LOUIS DESCHAMPS, · · · · Paris
>Medals, Paris Salon, 1877.

47   A Chacun Sa Part.

J. P. A. ANTIGNA (Deceased), · · · Paris
>Medals, Paris Salon, 1847-'48-'51.
>Medal, Paris Exposition, 1855.
>Cross of Legion of Honor, 1861.

48   The Convalescent.

D. R. KNIGHT, · · · · · Paris
>Pupil of Meissonier.

49   By the Seine (Poissy).

KARL P. DAUBIGNY, · · · · Paris
>Medals, Paris Salon, 1868-'74.
>Son and Pupil of C. F. Daubigny.

50   Early Morning.

A. MOREAU,   Paris

    Medal, Paris Salon, 1876.

51   **Anne Boleyn.**

CHARLES FRANCOIS DAUBIGNY (Deceased),   Paris

    Medals, 1848-'53-'55-'57-'59-'67.
    Legion of Honor, 1859 Diploma.

52   **Sunset on the borders of the Oise.**

J. L. HAMON (Deceased),   Paris

    Medal, London Exposition, 1857.
    Medal, Paris Salon, 1853.
    Medal, Paris Exposition, 1855.
    Cross of Legion of Honor, 1855.

53   **The Bird Charmer.**

J. B. C. COROT (Deceased),   Paris

    Medals, Paris Salon, 1838-'48-'55.
    Officer Legion of Honor, 1867.
    Medal, Paris Exposition, 1867.

54   **On the Seine (A Study).**

FERDINAND ROYBET,   Paris

    Medal, Paris Salon, 1866.

55   **The Page.**

W. SCHUTZE, · · · · · Düsseldorf
56   Little Gooseherds.

F. MIRALLES, · · · · Paris
    Pupil of Madrazo.
57   In the Parc Monceau.

L. KNAUS, · · · · · · Berlin
        Medals, Paris, 1853-'55-'59.
        Medal, Paris Exposition, 1867.
        Legion of Honor, 1859.
58   Le Salut des Amours.

J. G. JACQUET, · · · · · Paris
        Medals, Paris Salon, 1868-'75.
        Medal, Paris Exposition, 1878.
        Cross of Legion of Honor, 1879.
59   A Head.

HENRI HARPIGNIES, · · · · · Paris
        Medals, Paris Salon, 1866,'68-'69.
        Cross of Legion of Honor, 1875.
60   A Sunny Road.

J. G. JACQUET, ... Paris
    Medals, Paris Salon, 1868-'75.
    Medal, Paris Exposition, 1878.
    Cross of Legion of Honor, 1879.

61   Pauline.

A. L. DEMONT, . . Paris
    Third Medal in 1879.
    Second Medal in 1882.

62   After Sundown the Guards Home.

GEORGE INNESS, N. A., ... New York

63   Summer among the Catskills.

J. A. GONZALES, ... Paris
    Medal, Paris Salon, 1876.
    Grand Medal, Paris Exposition, 1878.

64   A Lady.

N. V. DIAZ, ... Paris
    Medals, Paris Salon, 1844-'46-'48.
    Cross of Legion of Honor, 1851.

65   A Landscape.

ALPHONSE M. DE NEUVILLE (Deceased), · · Paris
    Medals, Paris, 1859-'61,
    Legion of Honor, 1873.

66   The Bridge.

A. TOULMOUCHE, · · · · · Paris
    Medals, Paris Salon, 1852-'59-'61.
    Cross of Legion of Honor, 1870.

67   Leisure Hours.

R. EGUSQUIZA, · · · · · · Madrid
68   His Portrait.

I. DE LA MAR, · · · · · · Paris
    Pupil of Jules Breton.

69   The Favorite Flower.

ARTHUR QUARTLEY, · · · · · New York
70   A Marine.

JOSEF VILLEGAS, Madrid

71 The Standard Bearer.

ALPHONSE M. DE NEUVILLE (Deceased), Paris
    Medals, Paris, 1859-'61.
    Legion of Honor, 1873.

72 The Flag of Truce.

J. G. VIBERT, Paris
    Medals, Paris Salon, 1864-'68.
    Medals, Paris Exposition, 1867-'78.
    Cross of Legion of Honor, 1870.

73 Le Champs de Repos.

HARRY CHASE, New York

74 Coast of Massachusetts.

FELIX FRANCOIS GEO. PHILIBERT ZIEM, Paris
    Medals at Paris, 1851-'52-'53.
    Cross of Legion of Honor, 1857.

75 Venice.

WILLIAM H. HOLMES, - - Washington, D. C.
76   A Chioggian freight boat. Venice.

J. B. C. COROT (Deceased),   ·   · ·   Paris
    Medals, Paris Salon, 1838-'48-'55.
    Officer Legion of Honor, 1867.
    Medal, Paris Exposition, 1867.
77   Near Fontainebleau.

L. LHERMITTE,   - ·   · ·   Paris
    (The most celebrated charcoal draughtsman now living.)
78   A Sabot Maker.

H. BOLTON JONES, N. A.,   -   · ·   New York
79   The Summer Pool.

B. GALOFRE, - · · · · · ·   · ·   Rome
    Medal, Naples, 1876.
    Medal, Rome, 1877.
    Medal, Venice, 1879.
    Medal, Melbourne, 1881.
80   Near Naples.

EDOUARD DETAILLE,   Paris

    Medals, Paris Salon, 1869-'70-'72.
    Cross of Legion of Honor, 1873.
    Officer Legion of Honor, 1881.

81   **A Carabinier.**

J. P. LAURENS,   Paris

    Medals, 1869-'72-'77.
    Legion of Honor, 1874.

82   **Fredegonda.**

J. L. GEROME,   Paris

    Medals, Paris Salon, 1847-'48-'55.
    Medal, Paris Exposition, 1878.
    Legion of Honor, 1855.

83   **Majesty and Impudence.**

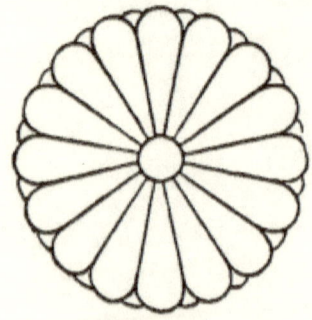

KIKU MON.

IMPERIAL (CHRYSANTHEMUM) CREST.

KIRI MON.

PRIVATE CREST OF EMPEROR.

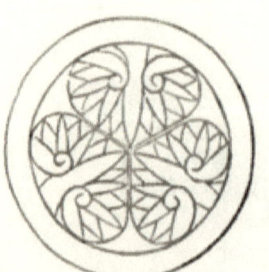

TOKUGAWA MON.

CREST OF THE TOKUGAWA SHOGUNS.

Keramics, &c.

INTRODUCTION.

The magnificent collection of Oriental works of art made by the *doyen* of American connoisseurs, and, in the sweet cause of charity, so generously opened to the public in Baltimore, was the incentive that led nearly all our collectors to study these beautiful productions. Among the number was the owner of this gallery, who, availing himself of the dispersal of the Brinkley and other collections, began the acquirement of the various objects I have herein described, the classification and arrangement of which have been a source of great pleasure to me. I have divided the Keramics into four sections, viz:

>   FIRST.—1-230. Japanese, and the unique collection of Japanese, Chinese, Korean and Cochin-Chinese Figures.
>   SECOND.—231-330. Chinese.
>   THIRD.—350-366. Korean.
>   FOURTH.—367. Cochin-Chinese.

The Chinese and Japanese ivory carvings and metal work, 400-427, I have placed under the heading of:

>   FIFTH.—Bric-a-Brac,

my aim, throughout, being to make the study of these interesting objects plain enough for a child.

Their owner is the first, to my knowledge, to plan a gallery in which both paintings and other works of art can be arranged without detracting from the beauty of or interest in either—indeed has accomplished what has been considered impracticable.

The descriptions of **the larger number** of the Keramic specimens are from the catalogue of the Brinkley collection, re-arranged, to include places of manufacture, and classified by Provinces; the others being compiled from the catalogues of the various sales at which the pieces were purchased, or from information supplied by former owners; foremost among whom was Mr. H. Shugio, whose contributions are initialed ("H. S.")

With regard **to** the dates, &c., **of** those examples with which no reliable information was furnished, I have consulted the MSS. of Brinkley's "History of Japanese Keramics," which valuable work will shortly be simultaneously published here and in Europe. Neither time nor pains have been spared in preparing the descriptions, which **I** have endeavored to make both concise and accurate; in all cases under rather than over-estimating the antiquity of the specimens; *the exact* period of manufacture being, in many instances, a matter of approximation. Marks, seals and signatures have when practicable **been** translated, they sometimes showing that the Chinese and Japanese potters, have in their anxiety to exactly reproduce **the** works of their masters, included even the signatures, and that the Hizen men had a weakness for using Chinese dates of the Ming Period. Therefore, **while a** mark is desirable, it is, by no **means, an infallible** proof of genuineness; besides which, many of **the most famous** potters, **like** Koyemon, never signed their productions.

It is yearly more difficult to obtain specimens of these "old masters" and the time is not far distant when the Japanese will be compelled to go abroad in order to study the works of some of their great Keramists.

EDWARD GREEY.

20 East 17th Street, New York.
    February, 1885.

PROVINCIAL GROUPING OF JAPANESE KERAMICS IN THIS COLLECTION.

*Names of PROVINCE, &c.	Pottery, Faience and Porcelain. Vases, &c.	Figures.	TOTAL.
Awaji (Is). *Tanshiu*.	3	1	4
Bizen. *Bishiu*.	1	13	14
Buzen. *Hoshiu*.	1		1
Chikuzen. *Chikushiu*.		3	3
Harima. *Banshiu*.	1		1
Higo. *Hishiu*.	4		4
Hizen. *Hishiu*.	33	12	45
Iga. *Ishiu*.	1		1
Ise. *Seishiu*.	2	1	3
Iwaki, Mutsu, Iwashi. **Oshiu**.	1	1	2
Iwashiro, Mutsu. *Oshiu*.		1	1
Izumi-Idzumi. *Senshiu*.		2	2
Izumo-Idzumo. *Unshiu*.	4		4
Kaga. *Kashiu*.	11	4	15
Kii. *Kishiu*.	5	2	7
Mino. *Noshiu*.	1		4
Musashi, *Bushiu*.	1	3	1
Nagato. *Choshiu*.	2		2
Omi. *Goshiu*.	1	1	2
Owari. *Bishiu*.	6	2	8
Ozumi. *Gushiu*.	1		1
Satsuma. *Sasshiu*.	7	6	13
Settsu. *Sesshiu*.	2	3	5
Suwo. *Boshiu*.	1		1
Tamba. *Tanshiu*.	1		1
Tosa. *Toshiu*.	1		1
Totomi. *Enshiu or Yenshiu*.		1	1
Tsushima. (Is). *Taishiu*.	3		3
Yamashiro. *Joshiu*.	35	29	64
Yamato. *Washiu*.	2		2
Made by Japanese Potters in Korea,	2		2
	133	85	218

*The names of Provinces in italics, **are derived** from the Chinese character for the first syllable of the native name, with **the affix of** *shiu* (province.) Sometimes both forms are in common use.

The Empire is divided into 85 Provinces, which include the Is. of Liu-Kiu and the Hokkaido (**Yezo** and Kurile Is.) leaving 73 home Provinces. Many of the latter lack the clays, etc., suitable for making keramic objects, while in others the attempts to found kilns have produced little worthy of notice.

This collection contains representative specimens from all the principal Provinces, and when those of Aki, Chikugo, Echizen, Sanuki, etc., (now on their way from Japan) are added, it will be one of the most complete and interesting in the world.

SECTION FIRST.

JAPANESE.

History, as recorded by potsherds rescued from the earth, proves that the antochthons of Japan made objects of clay four thousand years ago, and from legend and early record we learn how the ancestors of the present race, aided by Korean teachers, made pottery when Cæsar invaded England.

The fragmentary specimens of the more archaic wares, show little skill in technique; they being in fact mere "pottery infants" destitute of glaze and "possessing only the charms of a barbaric youth," and this description is equally applicable to the ancient productions of the Japanese, which, prior to the close of the eighth century, were unglazed and, even down to the thirteenth, insignificant and inartistic when compared with the pottery of the early races that inhabited our own continent.*

The reverence for antiquity, which is an inherited trait in all Eastern races, has led the Japanese virtuoso to place an extravagant value upon the works of their ancient potters and to regard them as superior to those of the great period, 1520-1871. This veneration has impressed itself upon connoisseurs and collectors all over the world and has generated the fallacy that the wonderfully quaint specimens made during the last three centuries were productions of the older period.

---

*Vide the admirable monographs of Mr. Wm. H. Holmes, published at the Government Printing Office, Washington, D. C., viz:

"Prehistoric Textile Fabrics of the United States derived from impressions on Pottery," 1885. "Pottery of the Ancient Pueblos," 1886. "Ancient Pottery of the Mississippi Valley," 1886, and, the most valuable of all to the student of Japanese Keramics; "Origin and Development of Form in Ceramic Art," 1886.

In 1223, a scion of the noble house of Fujiwara, named Kagemasa, popularly known as Kato Shirozayemon, later as Toshiro and by the artist-name of Shunkei, visited China for the purpose of improving the pottery of his country; which at that time resembled the rudest examples in the Korean section of this collection. He was absent six years and upon his return made tea-jars and other articles, for the æsthetic institution, *Cha-no-Yu* (ceremonial tea drinking) (No. 72,)—which, while almost worshipped by the dilettante among his countrymen, are caviare to most foreigners. After his death he was honored by the title of "The Father of Pottery" and a temple was erected in his memory where he is to this day worshipped under the title of "The Prince of Potters" or "The God of Kilns" and, twice a year, festivals are held in his honor.

The utmost that can be said about his productions is "they were an improvement upon the wares of his predecessors."

The record of the artistic Keramics of Japan really begins about 1510, A.D., when Gorodayu Go-Shonzui visited China to acquire the art of making porcelain; which ware forms, with pottery and stoneware, a Keramic trio, so interlocked that the history of one includes the other.

Porcelain was the dainty, younger daughter born into the Keramic family of Japan during the refined Feudal period; therefore, while we thoroughly appreciate and admire the rugged vigor, breadth and artistic feeling expressed in the productions of the potters who worked in the coarser material, we must pay the highest tribute to porcelain; foremost among which is Hirado, a production of a kiln in Hizen.

This collection contains a specimen of porcelain made by Shonzui (No. 11) and of an imitation of his ware made in China, (No. 300.) It is in fact an object-lesson to which the connoisseur, collector, and student can refer for standard examples of the productions of the famous potters and kilns of Japan, **and** proves that nearly all the delightfully quaint specimens we so greatly admire were made since 1600, A D.; the comparatively modern being, in many **instances**, the most artistic and interesting.

It is difficult to classify these objects Provincially, the native archæologists, who primarily, were our only reliable authorities, never having attempted such a task; besides which nearly all the records are histories of individual potters and their kilns, the Japanese never having worked in factories. The student also finds himself **utterly bewildered** by a multiplicity **of designations for** some of the specimens, which prevents many **persons** from continuing what is really a most fascinating **study**. These stumbling-blocks include, the maker's names (which have as many artistic aliases as objects in "Alice in Wonderland") names **of** kilns and ports of shipment, real and poetical titles of localities and places where the wares were sold, and the commercial designations used **by** Japanese curio-men; **added** to which are the, still **more** confusing, foreign, scientific names. I have therefore adopted Provincial **classification** solely on account **of** its being most intelligible to students, and to enable them to recognize, under any title, the ware of any Province.

The artistic influence of the potters who, during **the** three centuries they were practically isolated from **the** world, produced the admirable ware known as "Old Japan" has inoculated **their** brethren **in** Europe **and** this country; proofs **of which can** be seen in nearly every **American** home. The creations of these men, whose names may be unpronouncable to a majority of people, but whose works are mute expressions of their national feeling and love of the beautiful in nature, and who lived under social conditions that can never again obtain in their country, are exceedingly precious, both for those reasons **and as** mementos of the artist-artizans whose legacies have revolutionized the keramic forms of two continents.

The Japanese potter, unlike the Chinese master-workman, whose superb forms and glazes he aimed to excel, seldom subdivided the labor of production, and in most cases the man who threw the clay upon the wheel decorated the piece with brush or spatula, glazed it, and fired his work in a kiln built by himself. He often worked under the patronage of his Feudal Lord, whose refined tastes greatly aided his efforts and who sometimes honored him by assisting in his occupation; these causes and the spur of emulation created by the demand for tea-jars, bowls and other vessels, used in *Cha-no-Yu*, which became a potent factor in developing the potter's art, resulted in the production of the wares now so highly prized by persons of refined taste and which are carefully kept in museums and private collections, all over the world.

The long list, of these wonderful manipulators of clay, contains many names of men and one of a woman, whose works are treasured in this collection; among them being those of:

Nomura Seisuke "Ninsei,"	No. 94. and	Fig. 187.
Kenzan, - - - -	"	" 194.
Gozayemon, whose mark was		
"Banko," - - -	" 45. and	" 160.
Benshi, - - - -	"	" 171.
Kahei, - - - -	"	" 209.
Hokiu, - - - -	"	" 145.
Hozan, - - - -	"	" 201.
Kimura Sei-kin, - -	"	" 139.
Tomickichi, - - -	" 74.	
Hansuke, - - -	" 75.	
Sosendo, - - -	" 76.	" 175.
Rokubei, - - - -	" 108, 109, 110.	" 202.
Semba, - - - -	"	" 169.
Sampo, - - - -	" 33.	
Shuhei, - - - -	" 97.	
Dohachi, - - - -	" 114, 115.	

Shige-chika,	No.	Fig. 146.
Kichizo,	" 60.	
Hokikudo,	"	" 212.
Kaju "Mimpei,"	" 1, 2, 3 and	" 131.
Zoroku,	" 117.	
Zengoro Hozen "Eiraku,"	" 62, 63, 64, 123.	
Yusetsu, who used the stamp "Banko,"	" 46.	
Rengetsu, (Woman,)	" 126.	

of whom it may truly be said: Their art has "made the glory of Japan shine beyond the four seas" and that, prior to the revelation of their works, the foreign potter was completely ignorant of the charms of the unsymmetrical; of which, even to-day, he has but a dim conception.

Old **Satsuma**, that beautiful, ivory-like ware, can **scarcely be termed** a purely Japanese faience, being the production of Koreans and their descendants, who were kept apart from the natives in the Province of Satsuma. It only dates from 1598, A.D., and was never made in the form of large flower-vases, **or** incense-burners elaborately decorated with gods and parti-colored diaper-work. There **has** probably been more commercial-perjury concerning this ware than about any other in the world.

While all the **forms and** decorative motives used **by** Japanese potters **originated in China, or** were drawn from the source **from whence the Chinese** obtained their inspirations, it is no **less true, that the** first named artists modified and glorified **all they borrowed** from their **elder** brothers.

Japanese collectors, and **the** people generally, affix **the** term *yaki*: lit. "**baked**" or "fired," to all Keramic objects, exactly as we use the word "ware:" viz., *Awaji-yaki*—Awaji ware. *Satsuma-yaki*—Satsuma ware. Its employment by foreigners is pedantic **and unnecessary.**

33

1.—Cup, *Awaji Faience. Made at Iga, Island and Province of Awaji. H. 3 in.; D. 4 in. Date, 1830-40.

> Body glaze, cream white, crackled. Decoration a bunch of flowers and leaves delicately executed in green, black, gold, red, pink, and purple. Mark, *Mimpei*. Made by Kajû Mimpei.
>
> (*No.* 374. *Brinkley Collection.*)

2.—Bowl, Awaji Porcelain. Made at Iga, Island and Province of Awaji. H. 2¼ in.; D. 6 in. Date, 1830-40.

> Covered with a rich mustard-yellow glaze, and decorated with flowers and leaves in green, white and purple. Made by Kajû Mimpei.
>
> (*No.* 376. *Brinkley Collection.*)

3.—Bowl, Awaji Porcelain. Made at Iga, Island and Province of Awaji, H. 2¾ in.; D. 5¾ in. Date, 1830-40.

> Covered with green, purple, yellow, and white glazes, run in patches to imitate tortoise-shell. Mark, an illegible character in blue. Made by Kajû Mimpei.
>
> (*No.* 377. *Brinkley Collection.*)

4.—Incense Burner, Archaic Shape, with perforated sides (silver top) †Imbe Stoneware. Made at Imbe, Province of Bizen. H. 4½ in.; W. 5½. Date, 1660.

> A hard, reddish stoneware, the surface covered with impressed diapers.
>
> (*No.* 345. *Brinkley Collection.*)

---

* The Island of Awaji is off the Provinces of Settsu and Idzumi.
† Glazed Bizen ware is termed "Imbe;" unglazed, "Bizen." *Ninagawa Noritane.*

5.—Cup, Agano Faience. Made in Province of Buzen. H. 3⅝ in.; D. 4¾ in. Date, 1620.

> Covered with a dark-red glaze. (From the Collection of Ninagawa Noritane.)
> (*No.* 444. *Brinkley Collection.*)

6.—Vase, Himeji Porcelain. Made at Himeji, Province of Harima. H. 4¾ in.; D. 3¼ in. Date, 1840.

> Decorated with figure and floral designs in blue under the glaze.
> (*No.* 431. *Brinkley Collection.*)

7.—Bowl, *Higo (Yatsushiro) Faience. Made at Toda, Province of Higo. H. 3 in.; D. 7½ in. Date, 1630.

> Body glaze, a dark brown. The inside and outside have inlaid designs in white clay to imitate the marks of a brush. Copied from the Korean ware known as *Hakime Mishima*.
> (*No.* 354. *Brinkley Collection.*)

8.—Incense Burner, Higo (Yatsushiro) Faience. Silver top. Made at Toda, Province of Higo. H. 2½ in.; D. 2¾ in. Date, 1750. (H. S.)

> Very fine pâte, incised decoration of storks among conventionalized flowers filled with white clay, covered with a rich brown glaze.

---

* Higo faience is also termed *Yatsushiro*, from the name of the port and district in the Province of Higo, from which the ware was shipped.

9.—**Bowl and Cover, Octagonal, Udo Porcelain.**
Made at Amita-yama, District of Udo, Province of Higo. H., with cover, 3 in.; D. 4¼ in. Date, 1780.

Fine pâte, decoration, cranes and clouds in blue under crackled glaze. Marked, *Higo. Udo gori Amita-yama sei.* (Made at Amita-yama, District of Udo, Higo.) *From the De Jong Collection.*
These examples are very rare.

10.—**Vegetable Bowl, cylindrical, indented so that the section is a figure of eight.** Higo (Yatsushiro) Faience. Made at Toda, Province of Higo. H. 3 in.; Section, 3⅜ in. x 2 in. Date, 1820.

The body glaze, brown, flecked with blue. The decoration is inlaid, and consists of sheaves of rice in white clay. Mark, a cross.

(*No.* 360. *Brinkley Collection.*)

11.—**Wine-bottle, gourd-shaped, octagonal in section.** Blue and White Porcelain. Made by **Shonzui** Gorodayu in Arita, Province of Hizen. H. 8½ in.; D. 2¾ in. Date, 1520-30.

Decorated in eight vertical strips of various diapers, each alternate strip containing figures and floral subjects in white on a rich blue ground.
Shonzui Gorodayu (or Gorodayu Go-shonzui) a native of the Province of Ise, was the first Japanese potter to make porcelain. In 1510 he went to China and remained there five years, studying in Foo-chow and Kin-te-chang. On his return to Arita, he took with him clay, glaze, and coloring material, but when his supply came to an end the manufacture of blue and white porcelain ceased for awhile. After his death materials for making porcelain, were found within a few miles of his grave.

(*No.* 3. *One of a pair. Brinkley Collection.*)

12.—**Flower vase, trumpet shaped.** (The upper rim is surrounded by a fillet of silver with rich filigree work stretching into the interior of the vase to preserve it from injury. **Enameled Imari Porcelain.** Made at Arita, Province of Hizen. H. 23 in.; D. of neck, 10½ in. Date, 1650.

Decorated in blue under the glaze and colors over it. The centre is occupied by an irregularly shaped band surrounded by black lines, within which are flowers and conventional lions (*shishi*) in blue, red, green, and gold. Above this band the spaces are filled with diapers and floral designs.
(*No. 7. Brinkley Collection.*)

13.—**Plate, round, Enameled, Imari Porcelain.** Made at Arita, Province of Hizen. H. 1½ in.; D. 9½ in. **Date, 1700.**

Central design, red peonies with rich blue leaves on a white ground, surrounded by a deep border of green, red, and purple diapers, with medallions in red and blue.
(*No. 17. Brinkley Collection.*)

14.—**Bowl, round, Enameled, Imari Porcelain.** Made at Arita, Province of Hizen. H. 3¼ in.; D. 11 in. Date, 1700.

Outside, a scroll of chrysanthemums and *Aoi* leaves. Inside, a red ground with gold and white floral scroll, springing from blue chrysanthemums and separating large medallions with floral designs; the bottom is white with a central design in blue, *Shishi* and peonies. Mark, *Fuku*, (prosperity) in square.
(*No. 52 Brinkley Collection.*)

15.—Bowl, round, Enameled, Imari Porcelain. Made at Arita, Province of Hizen. H. 2½ in.; D. 8½ in. Date, 1730.

> Outside, fishes in blue and red. Inside, on bottom, three *howo* separated by medallions containing formal designs in gold on red ground. The sides decorated with rich combinations of diapers and medallions.
> (*No.* 49. *Brinkley Collection.*)

16.—Bowl, round, Enameled, Imari Porcelain. Made at Arita, Province of Hizen. H. 2½ in.; D. 8 in. Date, 1750.

> Outside, a green ground with *Howo* and dragon in white, gold, yellow, and red. Inside, landscapes, clouds, and purple and green diapers. Exceedingly delicately executed.
> (*No.* 25. *Brinkley Collection.*)

17.—Plate, square, Enameled, Imari Porcelain. Made at Arita, Province of Hizen. H. 2 in.; Square, 7 in. Date, 1750.

> Decoration, blue and red diapers with red and blue medallions. Mark, *Taimin Banreki Nensei.* (Copied from the Chinese mark of the Wanleih period.)
> (*No* 37. *Brinkley Collection.*)

18. Incense Burner, rectangular, with perforated sides and top. *Enameled, †Imari Porcelain. Made at Arita, Province of Hizen. H. 4½ in.; base, 4¾ in. x 4¼ in.; body, 3¾ in. x 3 in. Date, 1750.

> The sides have triple, lozenge-shaped panels, with raised designs of pine trees and clouds, and scrolls on a red ground. Round the edges are delicate red diapers. Inner portion covered with rich diapers and medallions with floral designs.
> (*No.* 45. *Brinkley Collection.*)

---

*Decorated with blue under and with colored enamels over the glaze.
†Imari is the name of the port from whence this ware was first shipped to Europe; hence foreigners have always termed it Imari.

19.—**Incense Burner,** rectangular, **with perforated sides** and top. Enameled Imari Porcelain. Made at Arita, Province of Hizen. H. 4 in.; Sides, 3¼ and 2½ in. **Date,** 1750.

> Sides decorated with flowers and butterflies, round which are bands of cherry-blossom diapers on red ground. **The lid is perforated in shape of coiled dragon.**
> (*No* 48. *Brinkley Collection.*)

20.—Bowl, round, Enameled, Imari Porcelain. Made at Arita, Province of Hizen. H. 2⅝ in.; D. 6½ in. **Date, 1750.**

> Outside, simple scrolls of dragons and floral sprays on pure white ground. Inside, covered with very rich decoration, viz., on the bottom a *Shishi* in yellow and red entangled in a net with white meshes on a rich blue ground. Round this are disposed medallions with floral sprays and *Howo* on rich green ground.
> (*No.* 50. *Brinkley Collection.*)

21.—Bowl. Enameled, **Imari Porcelain.** Made at Arita, Province of Hizen. H. 2⅝ in.; D. 3⅝ in. Date, 1750-60.

> Decorated, outside, with **rabbits** in fine enamels. Inside, a rabbit in blue under the **glaze.** Marked, *Taimin Nensei.* **(Copied** from a Chinese mark **of Ming period.)**

22.—**Bowl, with cover.** Enameled, Imari Porcelain. Made at Arita, Province of Hizen. H., with lid, 4 in.; D. 5 in. Date, 1780.

> Lid and body decorated with figure subjects and landscapes, delicately executed. Some of the figures are enclosed in circular medallions with rich red ground. Mark, on lid and cover, *Banreki Nensei.* (Copied from the Chinese mark of the Wan-leih period.)
> (*No.* 32. *Brinkley Collection.*)

23.—Bowl, round. Enameled, Imari Porcelain. Made at Arita, Province of Hizen. H. 2⅜ in.; D. 6½ in. Date, 1780.

> Outside, decoration very slight, floral sprays in medallions and flowers. Inside, covered with rich red glaze in which are medallions with floral subjects and between these the Sacred Jewel and flames in green. On the bottom, a landscape.
> (*No.* 51. *Brinkley Collection.*)

24.—Water-holder. Enameled, Imari Porcelain. Made at Arita, Province of Hizen. H. 11⅝ in.; D. 13½ in. Date, 1780.

> Decoration, a large medallion with a deep black border, containing a hawk on a perch, with curtains overhead, in red, gold and black; the rest of the surface richly decorated with peonies and chrysanthemums.
> (*No.* 60. *Brinkley Collection.*)

25.—Bowl. Enameled, Imari Porcelain. Made at Arita, Province of Hizen. H. 3½ in.; D. 8½ in. Date, 1780.

> Decorated outside with *howo*, fabulous animals (*Kirin*) and conventional flames, in blue, red, purple, yellow, and green, forming a scroll; inside, with a diaper of squares in red, among which are medallions with floral subjects, and in the centre a *shishi* and leaves in blue. Date, 1780. Mark, *Taimin Banreki Nensei.* (Copied from the Chinese mark of Wanleih period.)
> (*No.* 64. *Brinkley Collection.*)

26.—Wine-bottle, globular body with long tapering neck. Enameled, Imari Porcelain. Made at Arita, Province of Hizen. H. 8¼ in.; D. 4 in. Date, 1800.

> Rich decoration of sprays and flowers with circular medallions of diapers on a pure white ground.
> (*No* 44. *One of a pair. Brinkley Collection.*)

27.—Incense-box, double clove-shaped. Blue and white Imari Porcelain. Made at Arita, Province of Hizen. H. 1⅝ in.; D. 3⅛ in. x 3⅛ in. Date. 1800.

> The sides covered with diapers; top decorated with two *Howo* and bands of diamonds enclosing chrysanthemum petals.
> (*No.* 71. *Brinkley Collection.*)

28.—Incense-box, elliptical with straight ends. Form of the Hammer of Daikoku. Blue and white Imari Porcelain. Made at Arita, Province of Hizen. H. 1¼ in. Side, 3 x 2½ in. Date, 1820.

> Design, *Takara-dzukushi* (Collection of Treasures), in white on a blue ground.
> (*No.* 70. *Brinkley Collection.*)

29.—Vase, bulb-shape, with spreading neck, and crane handles. Blue and white *Hirado Porcelain. Made at *Mikawa-uchi* kiln, Province of Hizen. H. 8 in.; D. 8⅓ in. Date, 1740-60.

> Exquisite milk-white pâte. Decoration, pine tree and bamboo (emblems of longevity) in blue under a lustrous, white glaze.

---

*Termed Hirado, because, in 1745, Matsura, Daimio of Hirado, an island off the coast of Hizen, took the kilns of *Mikawa-uchi-yama* under his protection. *Mikawa-uchi*, is pronounced *Miko-chi* and *Mika-wa-chi*.

41

30.—Ash-holder, cylindrical with lid. **Blue and white, Hirado Porcelain.** Made at *Mikawa-uchi* kiln, Province of Hizen. H. with top, 4¼ in.; D. 2½ in. Date, 1760.

> Decoration, delicately executed landscapes in deep blue.
> (*No.* 107. *Brinkley Collection.*)

31.—Incense-burner, pierced lid and sides. **Blue and white, Hirado Porcelain.** Made at *Mikawa-uchi* kiln, Province of Hizen. H. 3¼ in.; D. 4 in.; base, 1⅞ in. Date, 1760.

> Lid pierced in the form of a chrysanthemum. Sides pierced to represent a bamboo basket with two reserved panels: "View of Fuji," and "Flowers and Sage." Inside, decorated with sages, etc., in blue.

32.—Water-holder, cylindrical. **Blue and white, Hirado Porcelain.** Made at *Mikawa-uchi* kiln, Province of Hizen. H. 7¼ in.; D. 6 in. Date, 1800.

> Covered with a boldly executed leaf scroll.
> (*No.* 83. *Brinkley Collection.*)

33.—Cup. **Blue and white, Hirado, Egg-shell Porcelain.** Made at *Mikawa-uchi* kiln, Province of Hizen. H. 2 in.; D. 4 in. Date, 1820.

> Decoration, eight vertical bands with floral subjects. Mark, *Zōshuntei Sampo-sei.* (Made by Sampo at the kiln called Zoshun.)
> (*No.* 110. *Brinkley Collection.*)

34.—Water-jar, bulb-shaped, with lid. Blue and white Hizen Porcelain. Made in Province of Hizen. H. 7 in.; D. 7½ in. Date, 1850-75.

  Lid plain. Body decorated with Chinese figures in blue.

35.—Perfume Box, irregular oval. *White Hizen (Hirado,) Porcelain. Made at *Mikawa-uchi* kiln, Province of Hizen. H. 2⅛ in.; length, 5¼ x 3. Date, 1700.

  Ground tamped, after glazing, to make it look like sponge or porous stone. Covered with archaic designs, representing plum blossoms, *howo*, dragons, cranes, bamboo, pine-tree, etc., with **red** overglaze in patches. All these forms are emblematic of longevity.

36.—Bottle, White, (Hirado) Hizen Porcelain. Made at *Mika-wachi* kiln, Province of Hizen. H. 10¼ in.; **D. 6 in.** Date, 1700. **(H. S.)**

  Unglazed. Body decorated with figures of **dragon and tiger**, modeled in relief. Vide Note to No. **35.**

37.—Water-Jar, Cylindrical. White Hirado Porcelain. Made at *Mika-wachi* kiln, Province of Hizen. H. 7½ in.; D. 6 in. Date, 1750. (H. S.)

  Decorated with conventional wave pattern, **carved in the** pâte, covered with a fine white glaze.

---

*"This variety of porcelain is very rare."—*Brinkley.*

38.—**Plate.** Enameled, *Nabeshima Porcelain. Made at *O-kawa-uchi* (Okochi) *yama*, kiln, Province of Hizen. H. 2 in.; D. 12½ in. Date, 1780.

> The central subjects are figures in a garden. The rest of the surface is divided by double red lines into eight panels in which are various floral and figure subjects. Colors, red, green, black and yellow over, and blue under the glaze.
> (*No.* 132. *Brinkley Collection.*)

39.—**Plate, with raised base.** Enameled, Nabeshima Porcelain. Made at *O-kawa-uchi* (Okochi) *yama* kiln, Province of Hizen. H. 1⅜ in.; D. 4⅝ in. Date, 1780.

> External decoration, floral sprays in blue; internal, conventional waves in blue and white, among which are two fan-shaped spaces containing floral designs in red over, and blue under the glaze.
> (*No.* 139. *Brinkley Collection.*)

40.—**Incense-burner,** dome-shaped, with sides and lid pierced in Genji crest. Enameled, Nabeshima Porcelain. Made at *O-kawa-uchi* (Okochi) *yama* kiln, Province of Hizen. H. 3¼ in.; D. 4 in. Date, 1820.

> Design, the seven flowers of autumn. Blue under and colored enamels over the glaze.
> (*No.* 134. *Brinkley Collection.*)

---

*Termed Nabeshima, because in 1716, Nabeshima, Daimio of Hizen, established the kiln of O-kawa-uchi-yama, the productions of which were entirely for his own use.

41.—Incense-burner, globular form, **Nabeshima, Celadon, Faience.** Made at *O-Kawa-uchi,* (Okochi) *Yama* kiln, Province of Hizen. H. 2½ in.; D. 3 in. Date, 1740-50.

> Covered with an exquisite soft green glaze.
> (*From the De Jong Collection.*)

42.—Plate, octagon shape, indented **at** sections. **Nabeshima, blue and white Porcelain.** Made at Okochi-yama (*O-kawa-uchi-yama* the hill within the great river). Province of Hizen. **H.** 1¾ in.; D. 9½ in. Date, 1780. (H. S.)

> Decoration, inside bottom, in a circular, reserved space. *Umé* **(plum)** blossoms, in white on a reticulated pale blue **base.** *Umé* **blossoms on rim.** Fine glaze, the surface of **which is slightly pitted.**

43.—Bottle, bulb form with tapering neck and spreading mouth, (silver top,) **Karatsu Faience.** Made at Karatsu, Province of Hizen. H. 15⅜ in.; Greatest D. 9⅜ in. Date, **about** 1480. (H. S.)

> Very hard, coarse, gray pâte covered with a thin coating of brown clay, in which are incised conventional forms of cherry and chrysanthemum blossoms and curious, vertical, spiral lines; the incisions being filled with white clay. The upper section is decorated with brush-made bands of white clay in Korean style. The whole covered with a heavy, bluish glaze, the lower part of which is crackled in patches.

44.—Tea-jar, gourd shaped, with lid. Iga Faience.
Made in the Province of Iga. H. 3⅜ in.; D. 3 in. Date, 1335-50.

Coarse, hard, granulated, reddish, unglazed pâte, covered with incised marks as though the surface had been " pecked " over with a sharp instrument.
Probably an attempt to imitate an old Korean faience.
Very curious and interesting specimen of ancient Iga-ware.
(*From the De Jong Collection.*)

45.—Cup. Banko Faience. Made at Kuwana, Province of Ise. H. 3 in.; D. 3¾ in. Date, 1770.

Body glaze, a reddish white, crackled. Decorated with archaic designs, flowers and a bird, in red and green. Imitation of the old Chinese painted porcelain. Mark, *Banko*, (everlasting.)
(*No.* 361. *Brinkley Collection.*)

46.—Wine-holder, with handle and spout. Banko Faience. Made at Kuwana, Province of Ise. H. 6½ in.; D. 6½ in. Date, 1832-5.

Covered with a grass green glaze running into rich blue round the neck. Made by Yusetsu Banko. Mark, *Banko*.
(*No.* 367. *Brinkley Collection.*)

47.—Bowl or Cup, of irregular form. Soma Faience.
Made at Nakamura in the Province of Iwaki.
H. 3⅛ in.; D. 3½ in. Date, 1840.

Hand molded, grey pâte. Greenish speckled glaze, flambé edge through which are seen brown speckles.

Decoration, outside in semi-relief, the tethered Horse of Soma, from the design by Kano Naonobu, and the *mon* (crest) of the Daimio of Nakamura, Soma Yoshitane, for whom this ware was named. Inside a galloping horse and stamp *so-ma* (together galloping horse).

48.—Cup, circular, with indented side. Izumo **Pottery.** Made in Matsuye, Province of Izumo. H. 2¾ in.; D. 4 in. Date, 1770.

> Body glaze, a brownish white, with roughly executed floral decoration in green, red, blue and white. (From the collection of Ninagawa Noritane.) This specimen illustrates the Izumo potters' earliest essays in enamel decoration.
> (*No.* 381. *Brinkley Collection.*)

49.—Cup, Izumo Faience. Made at Fujina, Province of Izumo. H. 3¼ in.; D 5⅜ in. Date, 1820.

> Body glaze, a brownish white, finely crackled. Decoration, floral subject in green, red, and gold.
> (*No.* 385. *Brinkley Collection.*)

50.—Tea-holder, **Izumo Pottery.** Made at Fujina, Province of Izumo. H. 2¾ in.; D. 2½ in. Date, 1830.

> Body glaze, yellow. Decoration, delicately executed floral design in green, blue, red, and gold.
> (*No.* 383. *Brinkley Collection.*)

51.—Cup, **Izumo Pottery.** Made at Fujina, Province of Izumo. H. 3½ in.; D. 4½ in. Date, 1840.

> Body glaze, milk white. Round the rim a band of diapers in green, red, yellow, and **blue** enamels. On the sides are delicately executed chrysanthemums in the same colors.
> (*No* 387. **Brinkley** *Collection.*)

52.—Plate, *Kutani Stoneware. Made at Kutani, (Nine Valleys) Province of Kaga. H. 1 in.; D. 8¾ in. Date, 1700.

Upper surface covered with a green glaze, in which are diapers in dark blue disposed round a flower and leaves in purple and yellow. On the rim are two strips of purple and yellow. The outside is yellow with black scroll. Mark, *Fuku* in seal character.
(*No.* 308. *Brinkley Collection.*)

53.—Incense-burner, square, (silver top). Kutani Porcelain. Made at Kutani, Province of Kaga. H. 3½ in.; square, 3⅜ x 3 in. Date, 1710.

Covered with a diaper of russet red: on the sides are reserved medallions, containing floral subjects, a bird on a bough, etc., in green, yellow, blue, and purple enamels.
(*No.* 319. *Brinkley Collection.*)

54.—Jar, with lid, Kutani Porcelain. Made at Kutani, Province of Kaga. H. with lid, 11½ in.: D. 6⅞. in. Date, 1710.

On the sides, large panels with rock and flowers; between the panels scrolls of vine-leaves and tendrils. Round the neck and base are bands of leaves and diapers in red. The colors of the body decoration are green, blue, purple, and red.
(*No.* 334. *Brinkley Collection.*)

---

* The common name for this ware is Kaga.

55.—Incense-box, cylindrical, Kutani **Porcelain.** Made at Kutani, Province of Kaga. H. 2 in.; D. 2½ in. Date, 1740.

 Body decorated with irregular bands of red diapers, between which are bamboos and pines in green and purple. On the top are rocks and plum blossoms in red, purple, blue, and green.
 (*No.* 325. *Brinkley Collection.*)

56.—Bowl, Kutani Porcelain. Made at Kutani, Province of Kaga. H. 3½ in.; D. 5½ in. Date, 1750. (H. S.)

 Covered with a dark, mustard-colored glaze, decorated with Botan (tree-peony) flowers, in blue, purple and green.

56a.—**Vase, with elongated handles.** Kutani stoneware. Made at Kutani, Province of Kaga. H. 10½ in. D. 4⅛ in. Date, 1750-1800.

 Decorated with archaic flowers, birds, *Shishi*, &c., in green and purple, under, and red enamels over the glaze.
 (*From the W. H. Hurlbert Collection*, 1883.)

57.—Dish, Kutani Porcelain. Made at Kutani, Province of Kaga. H. 3½ in.; D. 17½ in. Date, 1820.

 Covered inside and outside with a light green glaze, in which is a scroll of tendrils in yellow with chrysanthemums in blue.
 (*No.* 309. *Brinkley Collection.*)

58.—**Incense-burner, square. Kutani Porcelain.**
Made at Kutani, Province of Kaga. H. 2 in.
Side, 2 in. Date, 1820.

> Covered with a rich green glaze and black diapers. On each face is a reserved medallion, circular, with floral designs in red, yellow, green and purple. (From the collection of Ninagawa Noritane.)
> (*No* 317. *Brinkley Collection.*)

59.—**Dish, Kutani Porcelain.** Made at Kutani, Province of Kaga. H. 3½ in.; D. 15½ in. Date, 1830.

> A cream white glaze, the inner surface elaborately decorated with three *gumbai* (war-fans) and bunches of flowers and leaves in rich green, blue, yellow, and purple enamels. Round the outside a leaf scroll. Mark, *Fuku* in seal character.
> (*No.* 310. *Brinkley Collection.*)

60.—**Wine-bottle, hexagonal in section with rounded base** and neck. **Kutani Porcelain.** Made at Kutani, Province of Kaga. H. 5½ in. D. 2¼ in. Date, 1830.

> The shoulders have medallions containing coiled dragons in light red on a red ground with floral scrolls in gold. The body is covered with diapers in green and yellow. Round the base is a scroll of blue. Mark, *Shoreido, Kichizo Seisu* (Made by Kichizo at the kiln Shoreido), and seal of Tozan.
> (*No.* 324. *Brinkley Collection.*)

61.—**Cup, square, Kutani Porcelain.** Made in Kutani, Province of Kaga. H. 1¾ in. Square, 2½ in. Date, 1850-60.

> Fine decoration in red and gold. Marked, *Kutani*.

62.—**Bowl, with cover. *Eiraku** (Kishu) Faience. **Made by Zengoro Hozen** at Wakayama, in the precincts of the Castle of Tokugawa Harunori, Daimio of Kii, Province of †Kii. H. 5⅛ in.; D. 6¾ in. Date, 1827-35.

   Covered with a rich green glaze. On the outside are *Howo* and flames in relief, in yellow, blue, purple and white. On the inside, incised flowers. Mark, *Eiraku*. By Zengoro Hozen.

   (*No.* 269. *Brinkley Collection.*)

63.—**Bowl, with** spreading neck **and** narrow base. Eiraku (Kishu) Faience. Made by **Zengoro Hozen** at Wakayama in the precincts of the Castle of Tokugawa Harunori, Daimio of Kii, Province of Kii. H. 6⅛ in.; D. 7⅛ in. Date, 1827-35.

   The base is a rich purple; the body, yellow with archaic mountains and pines in relief. The inside is covered with gold leaf. Mark, *Eiraku*.

   (*No.* 270. *Brinkley Collection.*)

64.—**Wine-bottle, Eiraku** (Kishu) Faience. **Made by Zengoro Hozen** at Wakayama, in the precincts of the Castle of Tokugawa Harunori, Daimio of Kii, Province of Kii. H. 4½ in.; D. 3¼ in. Date, 1827-35.

   Ribbed horizontally; the edges of the ribs being green, the hollows golden brown. The bottom and inside are covered with green glaze. Mark, *Eiraku*.

   (*No.* 273. *Brinkley Collection.*)

---

*The Japanese sound of the Chinese Period Yung-lo—a seal conferred upon Zengoro Hozen by his patron Tokugawa Harunori.
†Kii.—*Kīshīu*.

65.—**Vase, pierced for hanging. Kairaku-yen Faience.** Made at Wakayama, Province of Kii. H. 6¾ in.; D. 3⅞ in. Date, 1827-35.

    Body glaze, a rich purple, with archaic designs in turquoise blue in relief. Mark, *Kai-raku yen-sei.* (Made at the Park of Ease and Fellowship.)
    (*No.* 400. *Brinkley Collection.*)

66.—**Vase, Kishu, Celadon, Porcelain.** Made in Province of Kii. H. 22½ in.; D. 11 in. Date 1830.

    Covered with celadon green glaze. The upper and lower portions are fluted horizontally and vertically. Round the middle is a band of peonies and leaves in relief.
    (*No.* 402a. *Brinkley Collection.*)

67.—**Saké-cup, Mino, Egg-shell, Porcelain.** Made at Ichi-no-kura, Province of Mino. H. 1 in.; D. 5 in. Date, 1810-25.

    Very thin, delicate pâte, almost equal to fine Hirado.
    Decoration, flight of geese crossing a mountain stream at night, in red and green enamels and gold. Rim of rich red decorated with black. Marked, *sei.* (Made).
    "The manufacture of this ware has always been confined to tiny tea-bowls or wine cups, whose outer surface is invariably plain, while the inner is decorated with designs of the utmost simplicity."—*Brinkley.*

68.—**Vase, cylindrical, with feet, pierced globular body, Tokyo Porcelain.** Made in Tokyo, Province of Musashi. H. 12¼ in.; D. 7 in. Date, 1880-5.

    Seiji, Celadon glaze with floral designs in blue and gold. Marked, *Seiji Kai-sha Sei.* (Made by the Seiji Company.) (No. 447.—"Old Chinese Porcelain."—Morgan Collection.)

69.—Tea-bowl, Hagi Faience. Made at Matsumoto, Province of Nagato. H. 2½ in.; D. 3⅞ in. Date, 1600-1625.

Cream-colored glaze, finely crackled, decorated with archaic figures of *Howo*, in chocolate-brown. This ware is known as *Ye Hagi* or painted Hagi. It was made by or under the direction of a Korean named Kikei, who lived first in the Province of Aki and afterwards moved to Matsumoto in Nagato, where he changed his name to Sayemon (Zayemon) and is known as Saka Korai—Sayemon, or Zayemon.

This ware resembles No. 771. Brinkley Collection, Korean, which was its prototype.

70.—Saké-bottle, bulb shape, **with** graceful, tapering neck, Hagi Faience. Made at Matsumoto, Province of Nagato. H. 9½ in.; D. 6 in.; **base,** 3⅜ in. Date, 1750. (H. S.)

Covered with a heavy bluish green, iridescent crackled glaze in which are minute gray specks.

71.—Flower Vase, cylindrical, Koto Porcelain. Made at Koto, near eastern shore of Lake Baiwa, Province of Omi. H. 9⅝ in.; D. 5 in. Date 1850.

Round the base and rim are bands of diapers, on the body figure subjects and landscapes in red and gold.

(*No.* 430. *Brinkley Collection.*)

72.—**Tea-jar, Toshiro-ware, Seto Pottery.** Made in Seto, Province of Owari. H. 2½ in.; D. 2 in. Date, 1225.

> Covered with a black glaze, slightly mottled. Made by Kato Shirozayemon, commonly known as Toshiro. (From the collection of Ninagawa Noritane.)
> (*No.* 410. *Brinkley Collection.*)

73.—**Vase, with swelling waist and trumpet-shaped base and neck, Seto Pottery.** Made in Seto, Province of Owari. H. 12½ in.; base, 3½ in.; top, 4½ in. Date, 1700.

> The body is decorated with a scroll of peonies in high relief. The handles are lion's heads with loose rings. The whole is covered with a yellow glaze, crackled. *Ki-Seto* (*Yellow-Seto*) ware.
> (*No.* 420. *Brinkley Collection.*)

74.—**Tea-jar, Seto Porcelain.** Made in Seto, Province of Owari, H. 3 in.; D. 2¼ in. Date, 1805-10.

> White, pâte with floral designs in blue under the glaze. Made by Tomikichi, the first manufacturer of porcelain in Owari.
> (*No.* 422. *Brinkley Collection.*)

75.—**Incense-box, Seto Porcelain.** Made in Seto, Province of Owari. H. 1 in.; D. 2½ in. Date, 1810-15.

> Decorated with archaic designs in white on a rich blue ground. Made by Hansuke, a fellow workman of Tomikichi and the best maker of blue and white china Owari has produced.
> (*No.* 423. *Brinkley Collection.*)

76.—Fire-holder, Seto **Porcelain.** Made in Seto, Province of Owari. H. 3½ in.; D. 4 in. Date, 1810-20.

> Covered with a rich chocolate-colored glaze, on which are flowers, leaves, and butterflies in green, blue, pink, and yellow enamels. Mark, *Yaki nushi Sosendo*, (Master-potter Sosendo.) Finely modelled. Sosendo was a fellow workman of Hansuke and was renowned for his skill in modelling.
> (*No.* 426. *Brinkley Collection.*)

77.—Tea-jar. Seto Pottery. Made in Seto, **Province** of Owari. H. 3⅝ in.; D. 3 in. Date, **1550-70.**

> Body glaze, iron red flecked with large metallic spots.
> (*From the De Jong Collection.*)

78.—Tea-Bowl. *Satsuma Faience. Made at Chosa, Province of Ozumi. H. 3¾ in.; D. **5 in.** Date, 1600. (H. **S.**)

> Fine, greyish-red pâte, covered with blackish-green and creamy white engobe glaze. Inside partly covered with a wrinkled greenish gray glaze.

79.—Tea-jar. Satsuma **Pottery.** Made in Satsuma. H. 2¼ in.; D. 3 in. Date, 1600.

> Gray pâte incised in Korean style and filled with white clay. Brilliant glaze.
> (*From the De Jong Collection.*)

---

*This ware is usually classed with Satsuma because it was made by potters brought from Korea by Shimazu Yoshihiro, Daimio of Satsuma, in 1598, who were settled by him in Chosa, Province of Ozumi, where their patron had one of his castles.

80.—Wine-bottle, square, with tapering, semi-gourd shape neck, Satsuma Faience. Made at Nayeshiro-gawa, Province of Satsuma. H. 9½ in.; Base, 5½ x 5½ in. Date 1680. (H. S.)

> Dense cream colored pâte covered with a finely crackled brownish glaze, upper part of neck decorated with conventional floral decoration in black.

81.—Vase, with tapering neck and handles. Undecorated, Satsuma Faience. Made in Province of Satsuma. H. 13 in. Date, 1700.

> Ivory white.
> (*No*. 160. *Brinkley Collection*.)

82.—Vase, square in section, with tapering base. Satsuma Faience. Made in Province of Satsuma. H. 5¼ in.; Square, 2 in. Date, 1720.

> The sides decorated with floral subjects: the shoulders and neck with scrolls and diapers. A piece has been broken off the base and replaced with Kyoto faience.
> (*No*. 150. *Brinkley Collection*.)

83.—Tea-bowl. Satsuma Faience. Made at Nayeshiro-gawa, Province of Satsuma. H. 2½ in.; D. 5¼ in. Date, 1800.

> Close, fine, pâte, covered with brilliant glaze, showing strongly marked crackles. Decorated in gold tracery with outlines of a lotus flower and the Buddhistic invocation.
> "*Namu Amida* **Butsu**."
> "Hail, Omnipotent Buddha," in gold. (H. S.)

84.—Wine-cups, two, Satsuma **Faience**. Made in Province of Satsuma. H. 1½ in.; D. 2 in. Date, 1810.

> Decorated with floral designs in colored enamels.
> (In a case containing two other cups, which are of crystallized jade.)

85.— **Incense-holder,** round, with lid. **Satsuma Faience**. Made in Province of Satsuma. D. 2½ in. Date, 1840.

> Delicate floral decoration.
> (*No.* 157. *Brinkley Collection.*)

86.—Bonbon Box, **with cover, Sanda, Celadon,** Porcelain. Made at Sanda, Province of Settsu. H. 2½ in.; D. 2½ in. Date, 1820.

> **Covered with a** light green glaze.
> (*No.* 406. *Brinkley Collection.*)

87.—**Vase,** with spreading neck and base, **Sanda, Celadon, Stoneware**. Made at Sanda, Province of Settsu. H. 8½ in. Date, 1830.

> **Covered with a rich green glaze.**
> (*No.* 405. *Brinkley Collection.*)

88.—Sweetmeat Dish, oblong. **Suwo Pottery**. Made in Province of Suwo. H. 1 in.; square. 6¼ x 5½ in. Date, 1700-50.

> Soft pâte, **curiously** decorated with purple, green and yellow enamels, **under a finely** crackled iridescent glaze.
> (*From the De Jong Collection.*)

89.—**Tea-jar, Tamba Pottery.** Made at Onohara, Province of Tamba. H 3 in.; D. 2¾ in. Date, 1620.

>Covered with a mottled glaze of brown and black.
>(*No.* 407. *Brinkley Collection.*)

90.—**Cup. Odo Faience.** Made at Odo, in the town of Otsu, Province of Tosa. D. 3½ in. Date, 1820.

>Body glaze, milk-white, crackled. Decoration in blue under the glaze; design, two figures under a tree watching a phœnix which flies toward them.
>(*No.* 445. *Brinkley Collection.*)

91.—**Jar, with cover, tapering base. Tsushima Faience.** Made in Is. of Tsushima, (Province of Tsushima.) H. with lid, 7¼ in.; D. 5¼ in. Date, 1700-1800.

>Covered with a thick lustrous cream-colored, curiously crackled "crazed" glaze; the crackles being irregular in form and following in some portions the lines of "craze."
>The inside and bottom glazed. The glaze and crackles of this piece strongly resemble those of Korean Cup. No. 355.
>(*From the Collection of Mr. P. L. Jouy.*)

92.—**Cup. Tsushima Faience.** Made in Is. of Tsushima, (Province of Tsushima.) H. 2 1/16 in.; D. 3½ in. Date, 1700-1800.

>Covered with a cream-colored, compound-crackled glaze. Very interesting specimen, closely resembling its Korean prototypes.
>(*From the collection of Mr. P. L. Jouy.*)

93.—Saucer for condiments, with scalloped rim. Tsushima Faience. Made in Is. of Tsushima, (Province of Tsushima.) H. ⅝ in.; D. 2⅝ in. Date, 19th century.

> Covered with a greenish crackled glaze.
> (*From the collection of Mr. P. L. Jouy.*)

94.—Tea-Jar. Kyoto Faience. Made by Nomura Ninsei in the environs of Kyoto, Province of Yamashiro. H. 3 in; D. 2 in. Date, 1660-70.

> Black glaze with an irregular band of white, producing the effect of a silk wrapper. The crackling of the white band is uniformly round. The **lower portion** is **unglazed**. Mark, *Ninsei*.
> (*No.* 177. *Brinkley Collection.*)

95.—Cup. *Kiyomizu Faience. Made in Kyoto, Province of Yamashiro. H. 3 in.; D. 5 in. Date, 1675.

> Body glaze, **a brownish white**. Decoration, a band of diapers in green, red and gold. **Mark**, *Kiyomizu*. (From the collection of Ninagawa Noritane.)
> (*No.* 237. *Brinkley Collection.*)

96.—Incense-box, round. Kiyomizu Faience. Made in Kyoto, Province of Yamashiro. H. 2 in.; D. 3½ in. Date, 1680.

> Body glaze, a very light green; decoration, three pine sprays. Mark, *Kiyomizu*. (From the collection of Ninagawa Noritane.)
> (*No.* 238. *Brinkley Collection.*)

---

*Kiyomizu-zaka. Name of a street on the slope of Otowa-yama, east of the old Imperial Palace, Kyoto.

97.—Tea-pot. **Kiyomizu Porcelain.** Made in Kyoto, Province of Yamashiro. H. 4½ in.; D. 3 in. Date, 1825-35.

> Decorated with figure subjects in green, blue, red, and purple enamels. By Shuhei.
> (*No.* 288. *Brinkley Collection.*)

98.—**Bowl, with four small lips.** Kiyomizu **Faience.** Made in Kyoto, Province of Yamashiro. H. 3 in.; D. 6½ in. Date, 19th century.

> Body glaze, a grayish white, over which is run, on one side, an irregular patch of dirty green and chocolate **brown.** Decoration, the seven flowers of autumn. Mark, *Yozo.* **Made by Yozo.** (From the collection of Ninagawa Noritane.)
> (*No.* 239. *Brinkley Collection.*)

99.—Cup. Iwakura Faience. Made in Kyoto, Province of Yamashiro. H. 2 in.; D. 3¾ in. Date, 1680.

> Body glaze, a brownish white. No decoration. A hard paste, almost stoneware. (From the collection of Ninagawa Noritane.)
> (*No.* 252. *Brinkley Collection.*)

100.—Cake-box. ***Iwakura Faience.** Made in Kyoto, Province of Yamashiro. H. 4 in.; D. 4½ in. Date, 1720.

> Made with a double shell; the inner solid, the outer pierced in various diapers. Cream colored without decoration.
> (*No.* 247. *Brinkley Collection.*)

---

*Name of the suburb of Kyoto, in which the kiln was situated.

101.—Incense-box, round. Kenzan Faience. Made in Kyoto, Province of Yamashiro. D. 4 in. Date, 1760.

> Decoration, bands of formal scrolls and diapers in black, in Korean style. Mark, *Kenzan. The son of Ogata Sansei.
> (*No.* 298. *Brinkley Collection.*)

102.—Wine-bottle, cylindrical, with narrow neck. †Awata Faience. Made in Kyoto, Province of Yamashiro, H. 8½ in.; D. 3 in. Date, 1680.

> The body is decorated with the seven flowers **of autumn**, delicately executed in green, red, gold and blue; the space above the shoulder, with a band of medallions containing floral scrolls. Crackle fine **and circular**. Body glaze, a dark buff. Mark, *Otowa*
> (*No.* 133. *Brinkley Collection.*)

103.—Wine-bottle, square, **with** narrow neck. Awata Faience. Made in Kyoto, Province of Yamashiro. H. 9 in.; Square, 4½ in. Date, 1770.

> Covered with a scroll of leaves and tendrils in blue, green, and yellow *engobe*, disposed about white peonies. Date, 1770.
> (*No.* 207. *Brinkley Collection.*)

---

*Ogata Sansei, called also Shinsei, Shinsho, and Shinsaburo, (a very famous potter, born in 1660), is commonly known as Kenzan and gave that name to this ware.

†Name of the eastern suburb of Kyoto in which the kiln was situated

104.—**Vase, square in section and tapering below.** Awata Faience. Made in Kyoto, Province of Yamashiro. H. 8½ in.; Side, 3½ in. Date, 1780.

> The upper part is pierced in a pattern of intersecting circles, in green and gold. Below, there is a broad band of blue enamel with medallions containing floral subjects. Body glaze, buff colored. Mark, *Ninsei*.
> (*No.* 185. *Brinkley Collection.*)

105.—**Vase, in the form of a ring, with high neck and spreading base.** Awata Faience. Made in Kyoto, Province of Yamashiro. H. 13 in.; D. 9 in. Date, 1780.

> Body glaze, buff colored. The front and back surfaces, decorated with medallions, fan-shaped on one side, squares with rounded corners on the other; the former containing floral designs; the latter, figure subjects and floral designs. The sides are covered with diapers. The decoration is in purple, green, blue and gold.
> (*No.* 231. *Brinkley Collection.*)

106.—**Wine-kettle, with spout and lid.** Awata Faience. Made in Kyoto, Province of Yamashiro, H. 4⅜ in.; D. 3¾ in. Date, 1780-90.

> Floral decoration, in blue; under, a very lustrous transparent glaze made to imitate delft faience.

107.—**Incense-burner, hexagonal, with ivory lid.** Awata Faience. Made in Kyoto, Province of Yamashiro. H. 2 in.; D. 3 in. Date, 1810.

> Each face contains a floral scroll in high relief on a ground of raised diapers. The faces are unglazed, but between them are bands of blue scrolls on a gold ground.
> (*No.* **222**. *Brinkley Collection.*)

108.—Cup, round, with flattened sides. Awata Faience. Made in Kyoto, Province of Yamashiro, H. 3½ in.; D. 5 in. Date, 1818-20.

> Body glaze brown; decoration, roughly executed pines, in blue, gold, and white. Mark, *Ninsei*. Made by Rokubei, to imitate Ninsei. (From the collection of Ninagawa Noritane.)
> (*No.* 196. *Brinkley Collection.*)

109.—Basket-shaped vase. Awata Faience. Made in Kyoto, Province of Yamashiro. H. 5 in.; D. 4 in. Date, 1818-20.

> Covered with a boldly crackled, reddish buff glaze. Mark, *Rokubei*. Made by Rokubei.
> (*No.* 197. *Brinkley Collection.*)

110.—Incense-holder, in the form of a bean-pod. Awata Faience. Made in Kyoto, Province of Yamashiro. L. 4 in. Date, 1818-20.

> Body glaze, buff with a red cloud. Decoration, leaves and tendrils in black. Mark, *Sei*. Made by Rokubei.
> (*No.* 198. *Brinkley Collection.*)

111.—Cup. Awata Faience. Made in Kyoto, Province of Yamashiro. H. 3½ in.; D. 4¾ in. Date, 19th century.

> Body glaze, buff colored. Decoration, the seven flowers of autumn, with butterflies. Mark, *Ninsei*. Made by Yebissei to imitate Ninsei.
> (*No.* 201. *Brinkley Collection.*)

112.—**Censer, hexagonal. Awata Faience.** Made in Kyoto, Province of Yamashiro. H. 3¼ in.; D. 5½ in. Date, 1820.

> The upper surface is moulded into the form of chrysanthemum with petals in blue, brown and gold. The lower halves of the sides are covered with diapers in green, purple, blue and gold. The upper halves are pierced in archaic patterns.
> (*No.* 189. *Brinkley Collection.*)

113.—**Dish, oblong, with** indented corners. **Awata Faience.** Made in Kyoto, Province of Yamashiro. H. 1⅜ in.; L. 8¼ x 4¼ in. Date, 1820.

> Decorated with formal scrolls and medallions in blue and red, to imitate Delft faience. Mark, a *Heron*.
> (*No.* 216. *Brinkley Collection.*)

114. **Cup, with narrow base. Awata Faience.** Made in Kyoto, Province of Yamashiro. H. 3½ in.; D. 4¼ in. Date, 1825-35.

> Design, the Genius of the Dragon (Chinnan Sennin) sitting beside a rock executed in purple, green and black enamels. Body glaze, buff colored, with reddish mottling in imitation of Korean *Gohon* ware. Mark, *Niusei*. Made by Dohachi.
> (*No.* 191. *Brinkley Collection.*)

115.—**Cup. Awata Faience.** Made in Kyoto, Province of Yamashiro. H. 3½ in.; D. 4½ in. Date, 1825-35.

> Covered with a black glaze in which are circular medallions with formal designs in red, green and gold. Mark, *Ninami*. Made by Dohachi.
> (*No.* 193. *Brinkley Collection.*)

116.—Vase, with cylindrical body, tapering below and spreading neck. Awata Faience. Made in Kyoto, Province of Yamashiro. H. 8½ in.; Date, 1830.

    The body below the shoulder is pierced in a floral scroll, and the part above the shoulder is decorated with horses in gold. Round the lip is a band of chrysanthemums. Body glaze, buff-colored.

    (*No.* 187. *Brinkley Collection.*)

117.—Cup. Awata **Faience.** Made in Kyoto, Province of Yamashiro. H. 3¼ in.; D. 3½ in. Date, 1830-77.

    Covered with a purplish black glaze. **The body is encircled** by two bands of interlacing medallions with formal diapers in green, purple, yellow, gold and red. Made by Zoroku.

    (*No.* 194. *Brinkley Collection.*)

118.—Wine-kettle. Awata **Faience.** Made in Kyoto, Province of Yamashiro. H. 6 in.; D. 4 in. Date, 1840.

    Decoration, panels, containing figure and floral subjects **in** brown *engobe*, in high **relief on an** unglazed paste in which a tesselated diaper is **impressed.** Between the panels and round the spout, base and rim, are bands of blue enamel. Upper surface decorated with floral scrolls in relief.

    (*No.* 223. *Brinkley Collection.*)

119. Tea-cup. Awata Faience. Made in Kyoto, Province of Yamashiro. H. 3⅜ in.; D. 5½ in. Date, 1870-80.

    Decorated with moon, flowers and snow, in white *engobe*. Covered with a dissertation on *Cha no-Yu*, (ceremonial tea drinking) in blue slip, written by Koho Fuhaku during the first part of summer, 8th year, period of Meiwa, 1771. Inside bottom, the character *Jiu* (happiness). On the **bottom, the** signature of the potter Shigen.

120.—**Tea-bowl. Raku Faience.** Made in Kyoto, Province of Yamashiro. H. 3½ in.; D. 4 in. Date, 1700-50.

A hard, brownish black pâte, covered with chestnut brown glaze, on which are three characters (unglazed).
"*Ni son in.*"
"Temple of two Buddhas."
(Ni-son-in is a famous temple on Mt. Ogura, south of Otago, near Kyoto). *Raku* means pleasure or enjoyment. The character engraved upon a gold seal given to Chojiro by Taiko Hideyoshi.

121.—**Wine-bottle, globular, with narrow neck. *Mizoro Faience.** Made in Kyoto, Province of Yamashiro. H. 8 in.; D. 5 in. Date, 1750.

Covered with a clear green glaze on which are maple leaves in red, blue, gold and purple, with a black trellis. The neck is a creamy white, with bands of gold, blue, red, and green diapers. Mark, *Gobosatsu.*
(*No.* 255. *Brinkley Collection.*)

122.—**Incense-box, in the form of a chrysanthemum, with pierced lid. Mizoro Faience.** Made in Mizoro, Kyoto, Province of Yamashiro. H. 1½ in.; D. 3 in. Date, 1780.

Body glaze a brownish white, with a band of scroll work and black lines. Mark, *Gobosatsu.*
(*No.* 257. *Brinkley Collection.*)

---

*Name of the suburb of Kyoto in which this kiln was situated. Mi (honorable) zo (muddy) ro (lake). This ware is also termed *Gobosatsu.*

123.—Cake-box, circular, **with lid.** Eiraku Porcelain. Made by Zengoro **Hozen**, in Kyoto, Province of Yamashiro. H. 2½ in.; D. 5 in. Date, 1840-50.

> Decorated with blue and white under the glaze. Design, five-clawed dragons, flowers and children at play. Mark, *Eiraku Hozen Konan ni seisu.* (Made by Eiraku Hozen on the south of the lake—*i. e.*, Lake Biwa.)
> (*No.* 281. *Brinkley Collection.*)

124.—Wine-cup, triangular. (Sakadzuki.) Kyoto Pottery. Made from a tile from the roof of the famous Ra-jo or Rasho Gate, Kyoto. The tiles of which were made 1200-1300. Made in Kyoto, Province of Yamashiro. H. 2½ in.; Side, 2½ in. tapering to 2 in. Date, (when cup was made from the **old tile,**) 1800-50.

> Coarse, dense, gray pottery, **on the sides of which are the characters** molded in relief: *Ra-sho-mon,* "Rasho Gate." Marked on bottom, in gold: "Tonoye. Senin."

125.—Tea-pot, in the form of a cha-tsubo, (tea-jar,) **and** other *cha-no-yu* implements. Kyoto **Stoneware.** Made in Kyoto, Province of Yamashiro. H. 2½ in.; D. 4 in. Date, 1800.

> Lid curiously cloisonned **in silver, with** blue and red enamels, repeated inside, over the spout. Entire surface covered with a violet glaze.
> Decoration, pine tree in gold and poem:
> " What is Cha no yu? (ceremonial tea drinking.)
> " It is the sound of the black painted pine trees beneath the winds breath."
> *By Ho-rai.*

126.—Tea-pot. **Kyoto Faience.** Made in Kyoto, Province of Yamashiro. H. 2½ in.; D. 3 in. Date, 1845-55.

> Made in the shape of a lotus calix, the lid being a leaf. Unglazed outside; inside covered with a cream-colored glaze crackled. Beside the handle are engraved the characters *Hachi ju san Rengetsu.* (Made by Rengetsu, of the Lotus, aged 83.) Rengetsu was a celebrated female potter of Kyoto.
> (*No.* 448. *Brinkley Collection.*)

127.—Oil-bottle. **Kyoto Faience.** Made in Kyoto, Province of Yamashiro. H. 4 1/2 in.; D ¼ in. Date 1870-1880.

> Hard pâte, covered with a grey glaze. Decoration in semi-relief, colored enamels. Rats carrying *daikon.* Bands of diaper patterns, in green enamel, about shoulders and below neck. Mouth overrun with brownish red slip.

128.—**Water-jar, with handle and spout. Kyoto Satsuma.** Made in Kyoto, Province of Yamashiro. H. 4½ in.; D. 3½ in. Date, 1875-81.

> Coarse pâte, crackled. Decorated with floral subjects in colored enamels and gold.

129.—**Bowl, with high base. Akahada Faience.** Made at the kiln of Akahada, near Gojo, Province of Yamato. H. 4⅞ in.; D. 6⅛ in.; Base, 3⅛ in. Date, 1810-20.

> Section cut from the base, in Korean fashion. Cream-colored glaze (applied by dipping the piece so as not to glaze the base). Covered with archaic designs of *Howo* and clouds in blue, red and green enamels. Band of diaper in red, above the base. Incised mark, *Seki-fu-zan* (Red-skin Mountain,) and seal, *Matsu* (Pine).
> (*From the De Jong Collection.*)

130.—Water-holder, with spreading neck, handles in form of a craw fish. **Akahada Faience.** Made at the kiln of Akahada, near Gojo, Province of Yamato. H. 6 in.; D. 5½ in. Date, 1830.

Body glaze, buff, crackled. Decoration, round the base, a band of green and blue diaper; the rest of the body covered with red diapers among which are reserved medallions with landscapes and floral subjects. The lid is covered with a rich brown glaze. Mark, *Sebi-fu-zan* (Red skin Mountain), and seal, *Matsu* (Pine) of *Akahada and Mokuhaku* kilns.

(*No.* 294. *Brinkley Collection.*)

MADE BY JAPANESE POTTERS IN KOREA.

130a.—Incense-burner, **cylindrical, tripod shaped, with silver top. Faience.** H. 3 in.; D. 3 in. Date, 1630.

A close-grained paste covered inside and outside with a cream-colored glaze very finely crackled. Round the body are plums, bamboos, and pines, delicately executed in light blue under the glaze.

Made by *Nakaniwa Moto* (called also *Moran*).

(*No.* 787. *Brinkley Collection.*)

130b.—Tea-jar. **Faience.** H. 2½ in.; D. 2½ in. Date, 1660.

A close-grained pâte covered with a reddish brown glaze flecked with cream-color. The piece is intended to represent a bag. Round the neck is a cord in black, and in the body are lines to represent plaits. Round the waist are three conventional designs in black.

(*No.* 789. *Brinkley Collection.*)

FIGURES.

The Japanese, "Historical Record of Ancient Matters" *Kojiki* (Published 611, A.D.), relates that during the reign of the Emperor Sui-nin, B.C. 20-29, clay figures were substituted for living retainers and animals, in the funeral ceremonies of Princes and Chiefs. From the remains of such effigies, found in various parts of Japan, it is probable that after this time the potters manufactured other objects than vessels for sacrificial and domestic use. These "earthen substitutes" are termed *hani-wa* "circle of clay" and *tatemono* "things set upright;" from the position in which they were placed about the tombs.

Keramic figures do not again receive more than incidental mention until the time of Koyemon, who lived at the beginning of the 17th century; whose works have been extensively forged. Since his day nearly all the famous potters have exercised their skill in modeling *ningiyo* "puppets" and these spirited objects have been produced at every kiln of importance.

This collection contains examples of nearly all the forms into which the ingenious potters of Japan have fashioned clay, and includes:

  Gods and demons,
  Famous persons,
  Mythical creatures,
  Koro, (incense burners),
  Incense-holders,
  Paper-weights,
  Okimono, (objects of art),
  Brush-rests,
  Hanging-vases, for flowers,
  Wine-bottles,

Netsuke,
  Tradesmen's signs,
  Votive offerings,
  Children's toys, etc.

The Chinese, Cochin-Chinese, and Korean specimens, are included, to show the origin of some of the forms used by the Japanese.

A number of the legends relating to these figures, were obtained from the scholarly works of Dr. William Anderson, of London, England, whose " Pictorial Arts of Japan," and " Descriptive and Historical Catalogue " of Japanese and Chinese paintings are standard authorities upon those subjects.

131.—**Figure of Oto Gozen,** (Otafuku), **Awaji Porcelain.** Made at Iga, in the Island of Awaji, Province of Awaji. H. 2½ in. Date, 1830-40.

> Face and hands unglazed. Hair black. Drapery yellow with floral scrolls in gold and medallions of diaper in green and red. Mark, *Mimpei*. Made by Kajû Mimpei. (From the collection of Ninagawa Noritane.)
>
> Otafuku, Okamé, Uzumé or Suzumé, is a famous personage in the Japanese mythology. It is said, when Amaterasu, the Sun-goddess, retired to a cave and left the earth in darkness, Uzumé assisted in luring her from her retreat by her dancing and singing. She is always represented with fat cheeks and a merry countenance.
>
> (*No.* 373. *Brinkley Collection.*)

132.—**Incense-burner, in the form of a Heron standing on an inverted lotus leaf. *Imbe Stoneware.** Made in Province of Bizen. H. 7½ in. Date, 1670-90.

> Slate colored pâte, fine as pipe-clay and almost as hard as porcelain. Finely modeled. Covered with a thin glaze.
> (*From the De Jong Collection.*)

---

*Glazed Bizen is termed " Imbe " unglazed " Bizen." *Ninagawa Noritane.*

133.—Figure of a Pheasant standing on a rock. Imbe Stoneware. Made in Province of Bizen. H. 8 in. Date, 1670-90.

Greenish gray pâte, lightly glazed. Finely modeled. Stamped "*Cho*" Long.
(*From the De Jong Collection.*)

134.—Water-holder, in the form of a Basket. Imbe Stoneware. Made in Province of Bizen. H. 6½ in.; D. 7 in. Date, 1700.

A greenish gray pâte.
(*No.* 349. *Brinkley Collection.*)

135.—Netsuke in the form of a rolling toy, St. Daruma. Imbe Stoneware. Made in Province of Bizen. H. 1½ in. Date, 1730.

Red stoneware, finely modeled decorated with gold. Glazed.

Daruma was the saint who converted the Japanese to Buddhism. Before crossing from Korea he took a retreat for three years, during which he wore his lower limbs off, through praying. The Japanese children make snow-men in this form, and the European rolling toy was taken from it. The Chinese version of the method in which this saint lost his limbs, differs from that of the Japanese.

136.—Figure of the famous Kyoto poet Dai Maru, (Hitomaru). Imbe Stoneware. Made in Province of Bizen. H. 12¾ in. Date, 1730-70.

Fine red pâte, glazed. Spiritedly modeled. Stamped "*Cho*" Long.

Kakinomoto no Hitomaru, was one of the famous thirty-six poets of Japan. He died, 724 A.D.
(*From the De Jong Collection.*)

137.—**Figure of** a Monkey making **Mochi.** Imbe **Stoneware.** Made in Province of Bizen. H. 3¼ in. Date, 1750.

Hard red pâte, brown glaze, mottled with grayish green. *Mochi* is a cake made at New Year. This figure is a satire upon the vigor with which the *mochi* makers pound the dough. The monkey is holding the beater the wrong way.

(*From the De Jong Collection.*)

138.—Incense-burner, in the form of a Cat sitting on a fire box, covered with a bamboo blind. Imbe Stoneware. Made in Province of Bizen. H. 6½ in.; W. 4½ in. Date, 1750.

A reddish stoneware covered with brown, speckled glaze. The Japanese cat usually has a tail like a rabbit's.

(*No.* 346. *Brinkley Collection.*)

139.—Figure of "Kanshin and the Impudent **Peasant.**" Imbe Stoneware. Made in Province of Bizen. H. 9¼ in.; L. 9½ in. Date, (De Jong,) 1700. Probably 1800-50.

Gray pâte, glazed with red, mottled in patches. Spiritedly modeled. Stamped, *Dai Nipon, Imbe to Kimura Seikin.* (Imbe pottery made by **Kimura** Seikin of Great Japan.) **Kanshin** (Chinese, Han-sin) was one of the "Three Heroes" of the Hau Dynasty of China. When he was young he was very poor but exceedingly ambitious. Rather than engage in a brawl with a bully in the market place, and thus sully his sword, **he** consented to crawl beneath the fellow's legs. He lived about **200** B.C. and was created a Prince. Although this incident is Chinese, it is often depicted by Japanese artists, etc.

(*From the De Jong Collection.*)

140.—Child's Toy, in the form of a Shishi (sky lion). Imbe Stoneware. Made in Province of Bizen. H. 1⅜ in. Date, 1820-50.

> Very hard, red, glazed pâte. Beautifully modeled, by hand, to imitate wood.
> *Shishi*, (sky-lion) an emblem of power. It is of Chinese origin and is often termed "The Dog of Fo."—*i. e.*, The Lion of Buddha.

141.—Incense-burner, in the form of a Shishi (sky lion) on a rock. Imbe Stoneware. Made in Province of Bizen. H. 8 in.; L. 10 in. Date, 1855-60.

> Red pâte, glazed to imitate bronze. Stamped, "*Ki*," to please. For description of Shishi, Vide, No. 140.

142.—Incense-burner, in the shape of a Boat, with a fisherman sitting in the bow. Bizen Stoneware. Made in Province of Bizen, L. 12½ in.; H. 5½ in. Date, 1700.

> Greenish gray pâte, unglazed. Exceedingly delicate workmanship.
> (*No.* 344. *Brinkley Collection.*)

143.—Incense-burner, in the form of an Ox standing on a corn-stack. Bizen Stoneware. Made in Province of Bizen. H. 5½ in. Date, 1730.

> Red pâte.
> The ox, *Ushi*, is the second sign of the zodiac and the symbol of the second hour, 2 to 4 a.m.
> (*No.* 351*a*. *Brinkley Collection.*)

144.—Figure of Yebisu, with Koi (Carp). **Bizen Stoneware.** Made in Province of Bizen. H. 7½ in. Date, 1800.

>Red pâte.
>Yebisu or Ebisu, one of the group of divinities known as "The Seven Gods of Good Fortune," was the third son of Izanagi and Izanami, the Creators of Great Japan. He is usually represented as angling for the red Koi and his figure is found on the *kami-dana* (god-shelf) and in shops and markets.
>(*No.* 351*b Brinkley Collection.*)

145.—Figure of the Genius Tekkai, seated on a Rock and blowing out his spirit. **Takatori Stoneware.** Made in Province of Chickuzen. H. 8½ in. Date, 1800.

>Covered with a rich glaze of green, **blue, white, and** brown tints. Mark, *Taka* in a circle, and the characters *Hokiu* (name of maker).
>Tekkai is one of the Rishi or Sennin (Taoist myths.) He is depicted as a ragged beggar, exhaling his soul **or** spiritual essence, in his own form, from his mouth. This materialization is sometimes represented **as** riding on the shadowy mule that has issued from Chokwaro's gourd.
>(*No.* 395. *Brinkley Collection.*)

146.—Incense-burner, in the form of an Owl sitting on a thatched roof. **Takatori Stoneware.** Made in Province of Chikuzen. H. 9½ in. Date, 1830.

>The owl **is** covered with an iron red glaze; the **roof** with green. Mark, *Taka* in a circle, and the characters *Shigechika* (name of maker).
>(*No.* 389. *Brinkley Collection.*)

147.—Figure of Chinese boy, seated, with fan. **Taka-tori Stoneware.** Made in Province of Chikuzen. H. 9½ in.; Base, 8¼ in. Date, 1700-1800.

> Cleverly modeled. Covered with a rich glaze of gray, buff, blue, and lustrous brown tints.

148.—Hanging-vase, for flowers, in the form of a Japanese lady carrying an umbrella. Enameled, *Imari Porcelain. Made at Arita, Province of Hizen. H. 12⅞ in. Date, 1700.

> Body covered with a heavy glaze, crackled. Costume, with floral designs in red and green enamels and gold, over, and blue under the glaze. Umbrella of dark brown. **Very rare specimen.** Made for the Dutch.
> (The head is not of Japanese porcelain; from the style of hair it was probably made in Holland to replace the original.) This figure was procured in the Hague.

149.—Figure of a Young Woman, in the costume of Period of Genroku, (1688-1704). Enameled, Imari Porcelain. Made at Arita, Province of Hizen. H. 6¼ in.; L. 9⅛ in. Date, 1730. (H. S.)

> Fine pâte, covered with a dense white glaze. Costume decorated with wistaria sprays in blue, red and gold, and with red and gold enamels. Hair, head-dress and eyebrows of dense black enamel.

---

*Name of the Port from whence Hizen ware was shipped.

150.—**Incense-burner, in the form of a Hare standing on a foot-ball, which rests upon a rock. Enameled, Imari Porcelain.** Made at Arita, Province of Hizen. H. 9½ in. Date, 1730-50.

The animal is covered with a white glaze, decorated with patches of black enamel, the foot-ball with celadon and the rock with red and blue glaze.

The *Usagi*, Hare, is the fourth sign of the zodiac and fourth hour—6 to 8 a.m. Seated upon the foot ball it is an emblem of pleasure.

151.—**Flower-vase, in the form of a Koi (Carp) leaping from the water. Enameled, Imari Porcelain.** Made at Arita, Province of Hizen. H. 9½ in.; Base, 3½ in. Date, **1750-70.**

Covered with a thick white glaze, decorated with blue under and red and green enamels and gold over. Imitation of old Korean ware. Base is impressed with a fabric.

The leaping *Koi*, is **an emblem** of vigor and perseverance. It is frequently depicted as ascending a waterfall, success in the endeavor being supposed to change it into **a dragon.** The origin of this idea is Chinese. When **the scholar (fish)** succeeds in leaping the **waterfall (difficult path of learning)** he changes into a dragon—*i. e.*, **becomes an official.**

(*From the De Jong Collection.*)

152.—**Figure of a Kyoto girl, carrying a puppy. Enameled, Imari Porcelain.** Made at Arita, Province of Hizen. H. 9½ in. Date, 1850.

The costume, which **represents the** old style of Kyoto, decorated with colored enamels and gold, over the glaze. Signed, *Zoshuntei Miozo*, (Miozo, whose artist name is Zoshuntei).

153.—Netsuke, in the form of a bearded old man, carrying the leg of a stork in his left hand. Enameled, Imari Porcelain. Made at Arita, Province of Hizen. H. 2¾ in. Date, 1870.

Glazed to represent ivory. Decorated with blue under and gold over the glaze.

(The *netsuke* is a toggle or button by which the *inro* (medicine-box) and tobacco box and pipe are secured to the girdle.

154.—Brush-rest or Paper-weight, representing a block of stone surmounted by the figure of a Shishi. Blue and white, Imari Porcelain. Made at *Mikawa-uchi yama* kiln, (*Mika-wachi*), in Province of Hizen. H. 2¼ in.; Length, 4 in. Date, 1850-60.

Decoration of base, *Chi-dori* and waves and on top *botan*, (tree-peony) in dark blue under the glaze. Figure undecorated

155.—Flower-vase, in the shape of a clump of bamboos, at the base of which are the seven sages. Enameled, Hirado Porcelain. Made at *Mikawa-uchi yama* kiln, Province of Hizen. H. 10 in.; Base, 8x10 in. Date, 1700.

The foliage is in blue, the bamboos are of light green and the dresses of the sages are blue and russet brown enamels. "The Seven Sages of Tsu" also termed "The Seven Worthies of the Bamboo Grove" were a famous club of learned men, who lived during the third century. They met in a bamboo grove, disregarded all laws and ceremonies, and passed their time in reading and conviviality.

(*No.* 125. *Brinkley Collection.*)

---

*Mikawa-uchi is pronounced *Mikochi* and *Mika-wachi*. This ware is termed Hirado because, in 1740, Matsura, Daimio of Hirado, an Is. off the coast of Hizen, took the kiln of Mikawa-uchi under his protection.

156.—Figure of Genius, with wine gourd. **Enameled,** Hirado Porcelain. Made at *Mikawa-uchi yama* kiln, Province of Hizen. H. 4½ in. Date, 1840.

> Decorated with yellow, **black, and** other colored enamels. This genius is one of the Sennin or Rishi, named Chokwaro, a famous Chinese necromancer, who could will a horse or mule out of his gourd and send it where he pleased.
> (*No.* 127. *Brinkley Collection.*)

157.—Incense-burner, in the form **of Baku.** White Hirado Porcelain. Made at *Mikawa-uchi yama* kiln, Province of **Hizen.** H. 6 in.; L. 5½ in. Date, 1780.

> Baku, is the genius that defends people from nightmare.
> (*No.* 123. *Brinkley Collection.*)

158.—Paper-weight, Lion (*Shishi*) crouching. White Hirado Porcelain. Made at *Mikawa-uchi yama* kiln, Province of Hizen. H. 2 in.; **L.** 3½ in. **Date,** 1820.

> (*No.* 118. *Brinkley Collection.*)

159.—Paper-weight, circular. White **Hirado Porcelain.** Made at *Mikawa-uchi yama* kiln, Province of Hizen. **Diam. 2 in.** Date, 1820.

> Delicately modelled chrysanthemums **on a** conventional stand.
> (*No.* 120. *Brinkley Collection.*)

160.—Incense-box, in the form of an Ox, lying down. Banko Faience. Made at Kuwana, Province of Ise. **L.** 3 in.; B. 1¾ in.; H. 2 in. Date, 1770.

> The body is covered **with** a golden brown glaze; the lower half of the box with a rich green. Mark, *Banko* (everlasting) (**Made** by Gozayemon before he was summoned to Yedo).
> For description of ox, vide No. 143.
> (*No.* 365. *Brinkley Collection.*)

161.—Cup, in the form of a mask of Tengu. Soma Faience. Made at Nakamura, Province of Iwaki. H. 4¾ in.; Base, 5¼x3⅞ in. Date, 1860-70.

>Hand moulded, gray pâte, translucent glaze, through which the speckled surface of the ware is seen. Eyes, eyebrows and mouth, colored in brown. Inside, two figures of horses *soma* (together galloping), from the design of Kano Naonobu.
>
>The *tengu* is a mythical creature, supposed to inhabit lonely mountains and forests. The ordinary *tengu* has a preposterously long nose and is winged, it usually carries a feather fan, of ancient Chinese shape. Children offer the *tengu* the worn-out brushes with which they have learned to write.

162.—Incense-box, in the form of a sleeping Fox, dressed in the robes of a Buddhist Bozu (priest). Aizu Stoneware. Made in Province of Iwashiro. H. 2¼ in. Date, 1881.

>Hard, gray pâte. Admirably modeled. Covered with a reddish glaze.
>
>Signed, incised, under base, *Meiji ju-shi shinki* (no) *toshi, moshun kakan. Aizu hongo, Kozan, tsukuru.* (Made during the last month of Spring, fourteenth year of Meiji, in the District of Aizu, by Kozan.)

163.—Figure of Genius Tekkai, seated on a rock, exhaling his spritual essence. Minato Stoneware. Made in Province of Izumi. H. 12½ in. Date, 1760.

>Covered with a honey-colored glaze. description of Tekkai, Vide No. 145.
>
>(*No.* 442. *Brinkley Collection.*)

164.—Figure of the Genius Gama, seated, with a frog on his shoulder. Minato Faience. Made in Province of Izumi. H. 16½ in. Date, 1800.

The face, breast, hands, and legs are unglazed; the rest of the piece covered with a light green glaze. Mark, illegible.

Gama Sennin is the Japanese title of a Taoist Rishi (mythical personage) whose familiar was a three legged white frog, *gama;* hence his name. He is generally represented as an aged man clad partly in leaves. The reptile is sometimes depicted as exhaling a vapor, in which appears the mirage of a walled city.

(*No.* 421. *Brinkley* Collection.)

165.—Figure of Dai-Koku, calculating upon **a soroban.** Kutani Stoneware. Made at Kutani, Province of Kaga. H. 7¼ in.; Base, 7¾ in. Date, 1780. **(H. S.)**

Heavy, coarse pâte, decorated with blue, violet, green and white enamels, and yellowish iridescent glaze. Costume decorated with *Daikon* (giant radish.)

This figure and Yebisu (No. 166) are masquerading as merchants making up their accounts for the New Year. Daikoku is one of the *Shichi-Fuku-Jin* (Seven Gods of Good Fortune).

Although garbed as a Chinese he appears to be a Japanese creation. Soldiers pray to him for victory, Buddhist priests have faith in his bringing them alms, and the people worship him that he may give them riches. He is often represented holding a miner's mallet and standing upon two **rice bales,** decorated with the thrice precious *tama* (jewels).

166.—Figure of Yebisu, examining a ledger. (Companion to Daikoku). Kutani Stoneware. Made at Kutani, Province of Kaga. H. 7¾ in.; Base, 6¼ in. Date, 1780. **(H. S.)**

Heavy, coarse pâte, decorated with blue, violet, green and white enamels and yellowish, iridescent glaze.

Costume decorated with *koi* (carp) and bamboo. For description of Yebisu vide No. 144.

167.—Incense-box, in the form of a sleeping Duck. **Kutani Stoneware.** Made at Kutani, Province of Kaga. L. 3 in.; Base, 2 in. Date, 1830.

> Covered with yellow, blue and green enamels.
> (*No.* 320. *Brinkley Collection.*)

168.—Incense-box, in the form of a Sparrow. **Kutani Porcelain.** Made at Kutani, Province of Kaga. L. 3 in.; Base, 2¾ in. Date, 1830.

> The lower half is covered with blue enamel, on which are floral designs in yellow, green and purple; the feathers of the bird are in russet red.
> (*No.* 322. *Brinkley Collection.*)

169.—Figure of Genius and Rat. **Kishiu Porcelain.** Made at Otoko-yama kiln, Province of Kii. H. 6½ in. Date, 1820.

> Covered with celadon (green) glaze. Mark, *Nanki Otoko-yama* in blue (*Nanki* is another name for Kishiû), and the characters *Sem-ba* in a circle (maker's name).
> (*No.* 399. *Brinkley Collection.*)

170.—Sweetmeat dish, with cover, in the form of fringe-tailed, longevity Tortoise. **Kishiu Porcelain.** Made at Otoko yama kiln, Province of Kii. H. with cover, 5 in.; L. 11½ in. Date, 1820.

> Decorated with blue, under glaze. Marked, under the fringe, "*Nanki Otokoyama.*" (*Nanki* is another name for Province of Kii. Kishiu.)
> The fringe-tailed tortoise, emblematic of long-life, is of Chinese origin. Living specimens of this mythical creature are "manufactured" by inserting a miniature eel-grass under the shell of the water tortoise, which soon grows a long fringe of the weed. An image of the fringe-tailed tortoise is used at Japanese wedding ceremonies.

171.—Votive offering. Group, "Seven Gods of Happiness." Imado (Tokyo) Faience. Province of Musashi. H. 3½ in.; W. 4 in. Date, 1772.

> Black clay, unglazed. Inscription on the bottom *An-yei gan-nen sho-gwattsu heshi su* (reventially offered up in the first month of the first year of Anyei, *i. e.*, 1772). Inscription on back *Tenka Taihei Kokka ansei Utokujin Kaiun shussei, Nikkwo*. This inscription is stamped inside a circle. It signifies:—"Offered to the fortune-giving God of Nikkwo, as a supplication for peace and happiness, national and domestic, and personal fortune and advancement." Beside the circle are the characters *Benshi* (name of maker).
> (*No.* 441. *Brinkley Collection.*)

172.—Figure of an Old Man, seated on a rock. Tokyo Pottery. Province of Musashi. H. 5½ in. Date, 1870.

> Unglazed and intended to imitate a wood carving. Made by Hattori Tsuna, commonly called Korea, an artist of Tôkyô.
> (*No.* 446. *Brinkley Collection.*)

173.—Child's toy. Figure of Rakan Batsudara, seated on a rock, with his tiger. Tokyo Pottery. Province of Musashi. H. 3 in. Date, 1880.

> Face, hands, and limbs, of Rakan, unglazed. The costume, etc., of the figure and the rock and tiger covered with colored enamels, glazed.
> Batsudara was a magician who became one of the sixteen Rakan (arhats) Beloved Disciples of Buddha. He is usually depicted, seated on a rock with a tiger crouching at his feet. Sometimes he holds a *shakujo* (ringed staff).

174.—**Figure of an old Woman with a basket.** Shigaraki Stoneware. Made at Nagano-mura, Province of Omi. H. 8½ in. Date, 1770.

> The face, arms, and legs unglazed; the rest of the piece covered with a light buff glaze, sparsely decorated with black.
> This figure is a satire upon professional mendicancy. The woman's pinched face and agonized expression contrasting with her well filled wallet.
> (*No.* 440. *Brinkley Collection.*)

175.—**Square Seal, with Kirin (Japanese Unicorn) for handle.** Seto Porcelain. Made in Seto, Province of Owari. H. 3¼ in.; Square, 3 in. Date, 1810-20.

> Finely modeled by Sosendo, a fellow workman of Hansuke, renowned for his skill in modelling.
> The *Kirin* (Chinese *Kilin*) is a supernatural animal having a deer-like form, one horn and flame-like appendages. It is of Chinese origin, is an emblem of good, and represents the two principles of nature *K'i* (male) *lin* (female).
> (*No.* 424. *Brinkley Collection.*)

176.—**Models of houses, (two), used in miniature landscapes.** Seto Porcelain. Made in Seto, Province of Owari. Dwelling house, H. 3⅜ in.; L. 6⅜ in. Out-buildings, H. 3⅜ in.; L. 4 in. Date, 1830-50.

> Hard pâte, covered with a bluish-white glaze, decorated with blue, green, and brown enamels.
> These miniature objects are most effectively used by the Japanese in their wonderful dwarf landscapes.

177.—**Paper-weight, in the form of camelia leaves and bud.** Satsuma Faience. Made in the Province of Satsuma. H. 2 in.; L. 6½ in. Date, 1810.

> Covered with a green and blue glaze.
> (*No.* 153. *Brinkley Collection.*)

178.—Figure of Confucius, seated upon a rock, reading a book. Satsuma Faience. Made in Province of Satsuma. H. 10½ in. Date, according to Dr. De Jong, 1600-50. (Probably, 1830-40.)

> Crackle larger than that of No. 179. Decoration, dragons and clouds in blue, green, brown and yellow enamels.
> Confucius, the famous Chinese sage, founded the present political system of the Empire.
> *(From the De Jong Collection.)*

179.—Figure of Hotei, seated upon his bag holding a bell in his right hand. Satsuma Faience. Made in Province of Satsuma. H. 8½ in. Date, according to Dr. De Jong, 1728. (Probably, 1830-40).

> Covered with finely **crackled** glaze. Costume, etc., **decorated** with green, blue and red enamels and gold.
> Hotei, the St. Nicholas of the Japanese, is one of the "Seven Gods of Good Fortune." He is supposed to have been a Chinese priest, famed for his fatness and for his love of children. He delighted in playing with them and would often predict their future. Named Hotei from *ho* (cloth) and *tei* (bag) the cloth-bag he always carried.
> *There are many versions of the story of Hotei* **Sama**.
> *(From the De Jong Collection.)*

180.—Figure of longevity, fringe-tailed Tortoise, upon a rock. Satsuma Faience. Made in Province of Satsuma. H. 8½ in. Date, 1830-40.

> Decoration, blue, red and green enamels and gold.
> For description of longevity tortoise, vide No. 170.

181.—Group. "The Three Wine Tasters round the Saké Jar." Satsuma Faience. Made in Province of Satsuma. H. 7½ in. Date, 1850.

    (Purchased by Dr. De Jong in 1860).
    Very fine, hard pâte, decorated with blue, red, and green enamels and gold.
    The three wine tasters, Buddha, Laotze and Confucius, typify the three beliefs, Buddhism, Taoism and Confucianism. The idea being that although the forms of their beliefs differ they are the result of a common inspiration.
    (*From the De Jong Collection.*)

182.—Incense-box. Figure of a Boy, resting, with a bundle over his shoulder. Satsuma Faience. Made in Province of Satsuma. H. 1⅞ in. Date, 1865-70.

    Decoration, colored enamels and gold.

183.—Figure of Hotei, with bag and children. Sanda Stoneware. Made in Province of Settsu. H. 10 in. Date, 1700.

    Celadon. The face, arms, and breast are unglazed. The rest of the piece covered with a sea-green glaze.
    For description of Hotei, Vide No. 179.
    (*No.* 403. *Brinkley Collection.*)

184.—Paper-weight, in the form of a Tortoise. Miuso Pottery. Made in Province of Settsu. H. 2¾ in.; L. 6½ in. Date, 1848.

    Soft pâte. Under shell, rich chocolate-colored glaze, with incised white lines. Upper shell, curious, iridescent yellow glaze. Marked, *Kiko*.
    The Kame (tortoise) is an emblem of longevity.

185.—Figure of Genius, seated, with a Dragon coiled about his seat. Kobe Pottery. Province of Settsu. H. 7½ in. Date, 1880.

> Covered with turquoise blue and purple glazes. **Face, hands and feet unglazed.**
> (*No.* 447. *Brinkley Collection.*)

186.—Figure of Hotei, with bag. **Shidoro Stoneware.** Made in Province of Totomi. H. 8 in.; W. 7 in. Date, 1770.

> **Covered with** brown glaze spotted with **black.** (From the collection of Ninagawa Noritane).
> **For** description of Hotei, Vide No. 179.
> (*No.* 433. *Brinkley Collection.*)

187.—Incense-holder, in the form of a Mallard sleeping. Kyoto Faience. Made by Nomura Ninsei in the environs of Kyoto, Province of Yamashiro. H. 2 in.; L. 3¾ in. Date, 1660-70.

> **The feathers are in blue,** gold, green and **black. Very fine** crackle and reddish white glaze. Mark, *Ninsei*.
> (*No.* 176. *Brinkley Collection.*)

188.—Incense-burner, in the form of Hotei, reclining. Kiyomizu Faience, Made in Kyoto, Province of Yamashiro. L. 11 in.; H. 6⅞ in. Date, 1500-1600.

> Admirably modeled.
> Face, hands and body partly glazed. Costume and bag covered with a heavy grayish, crackled glaze, decorated with colored enamels in diapers, *partly incised, in old Korean style.*
> Pâte of dense clay, so hard that it resembles porcelain.
> *Considered by Dr. Louis De Jong to be a specimen of old Karatsu. Date,* 1450-1500.
> These figures are very rare.
> Cover of the bag, pieced brass. Marks, (unknown).
> For description of Hotei, Vide No. 179.
> (*From the De Jong Collection.*)

189.—**Flower-vase, in the form of Otafuku dancing. Kiyomizu Stoneware.** Made in Kyoto, Province of Yamashiro. H. 12½ in.; Base, 5½ in. Date, 1690. (H. S.)

Very close, hard, gray pâte, decorated with black and gray in patches. Covered with a lustrous crackled glaze.

For description of Otafuku, Otogozen, Okami, Uzumi or Suzume, Vide No. 131.

190.—**Incense-burner, in the form of** a Shishi, (sky-lion) crouching. *Kiyomizu Faience. Made in Kyoto, Province of Yamashiro. H. 5½ in.; L. 8½ in. Date, 1700.

Body glaze, a grayish white; salient lines touched with dark brown glaze.

For description of *Shishi*, Vide No. 140.

(*No.* 241. *Brinkley Collection.*)

191.—**Figure of Daikoku sitting on a Rice-mortar. Awata Faience.** Made in Kyoto, Province of Yamashiro. H. 9½ in. Date, 1680.

Cleverly modeled. The drapery richly enameled in gold, blue and green.

(*No.* 179. *Brinkley Collection.*)

192.—**Two Figures, Goro and Asaina, the latter, attempting to restrain the former, pulls the skirt off his armor. Awata Faience.** Made in Kyoto, Province of Yamashiro. H. 10 in. and 15 in., respectively. Date, 1680.

Decorated with blue, yellow, green and gold enamels. Admirably modeled. The trial of strength between the famous Soga no Goro and Asaina Saburo, is a favorite subject with the Japanese potter and artist.

(*No.* 231*b*. *Brinkley Collection.*)

---

*Kiyomizu-zaka. Name of a street on the slope of Otowa-yama, east of the old Imperial Palace, Kyoto.

193.—Incense-holder, in the form of a sleeping Goose. **Awata Faience.** Made in Kyoto, Province of Yamashiro. L. 3½ in.; **H.** 2¼ in. Date, 1700-20.

Feathers of starch blue, neck and body of lustrous green enamel, over a heavy, crackled glaze.
Mark, *Ninsei*. (Forgery, but a good, old piece).
(*From the De Jong Collection.*)

194.—Figure of Otafuku, the Japanese Venus. **Awata Faience.** Made in Kyoto, Province of Yamashiro. H. 8 in. Date, 1730-**50.**

Face and hands unglazed; **hair** black; drapery **decorated** with maple leaves in yellow, green, and red, and diapers in black. (From the collection of Ninagawa **N**oritane).
Signed, *Kenzan*. Made by Kenzan.
(*No.* 299a. *Brinkley Collection.*)

195.—Incense-burner, **in the form of** a Tiger seated on a rock. **Awata Faience.** Made in Kyoto, Province of Yamashiro. H. 10 in. Date, 1700-50.

Animal of gray **faience, covered** with a heavy, brilliant, iridescent **glaze, curiously crazed.** Stomach white, rest of the figure **yellow, with brown stripes.** (Korean style.) Eyes of **green, and mouth, etc., of red enamel.** Rock of red faience covered with dull brown enamel.

The tiger, *Tora*, is the third sign of the zodiac and the symbol of the third hour—4 to 6 a.m.

196.—Incense-burner, figure of Yebisu riding upon a Carp. **Awata Faience.** Made in Kyoto, Province of Yamashiro. H. 9½ in.; L. 10 in. Date, 1750.

The fish is red; the face, hands and legs of the god are unglazed; his clothes are in red, yellow, and green enamels with diapers.
For description of Yebisu, Vide No. 144.
(*No.* 224. *Brinkley Collection.*)

197.—**Figure of the Poet Hitomaru, seated. Awata Faience.** Made in Kyoto, Province of Yamashiro. H. 8 in. Date, 1780.

Drapery richly decorated with green, blue, and gold scrolls, floral medallions and diapers. Crackle fine. Body glaze, buff colored.

For description of Hitomaru, Vide No. 136.

(*No.* 183. *Brinkley Collection.*)

198.—**Figure of Hotei and Child, with a Bag which forms a vessel for washing the wine cup. Awata Faience.** Made in Kyoto, Province of Yamashiro. H. 7½ in.; Breadth, 6 in. Date, 1780.

The face, breast, and hands of the god are unglazed; the rest of the piece is decorated with blue and green enamels and gold.

For description of Hotei, Vide No. 179.

This figure represents the god as endeavoring to entice a child into his bag.

(*No.* 225. *Brinkley Collection.*)

199.—**Figure of Hotei and Child, forming an incense-burner. Awata Faience.** Made in Kyoto, Province of Yamashiro. H. 4 in.; L. 5 in. Date, 1780.

Head, breast, and arms of god are unglazed; the rest of the group, covered with light gray glaze and sparse floral decoration in black.

For description of Hotei, Vide No. 179.

(*No.* 231 *d. Brinkley Collection.*)

200.—**Incense-box, in the form of a sleeping Ox. Awata Faience.** Made in Kyoto, Province of Yamashiro. L. 2⅞ in.; H. 2 in. Date, 1780-1800.

Covered with a delicate, pale green, crackled glaze. Mark obscure.

(*From the De Jong Collection.*)

201.—Hanging flower-vase, round. **Awata Faience.** Made in Kyoto, Province of Yamashiro. D. 5 in. Date, 1800.

Body glaze a greenish brown. Design, an old man seated under a tree, a rock, and waterfall in high relief. Mark, *Hozan*.
(*No.* 231 *l. Brinkley Collection.*)

202.—**Figure of** Genius with Gourd. Awata Faience. Made in Kyoto, Province of Yamashiro. H. 5½ in. Date, 1818.

Covered with a greenish brown glaze, except the face and one arm, which are unglazed. Mark, *Rokubei*. Made by Rokubei.
This figure represents the Sennin or Rishi Chokwaro. For description, Vide No. 156.
(*No.* 199. *Brinkley Collection.*)

203.—**Figure of** Hotei, **dancing. Awata Faience.** Made in Kyoto, Province of Yamashiro. H. 7½ in. Date, 1850.

The upper part of the figure is unglazed, the drapery of the lower part is in red, green, black, and slate-colored enamels. For description of Hotei, Vide No. 179.
(*No.* 184. *Brinkley Collection.*)

204.—Figure **of a Tengu** emerging from its shell. Kyoto Faience. Made in Kyoto, Province of Yamashiro. L. 7½ in.; H. 5¾ in. Date, 1850-60.

Hard, gray pâte covered with a brilliant glaze, flambé on the wings and face. Stamp, obscure.
The Japanese use the expression "a tengu's egg" **as we do** "a mare's nest."
For description of Tengu, Vide No. 161.

205.—Figure of the Rakan Nagasaina, holding his Bowl. Kyoto Faience. Made in Kyoto, Province of Yamashiro. H. 4¼ in. Date, 1875-80.

    Hard, gray pâte, covered with a heavy glaze coarsely decorated with red, blue, black and green enamels, and gold. The Rakan Nagasaina was a magician converted by Amida Buddha, who made him one of his sixteen Rakan, (Arhats) beloved disciples. He is usually depicted as holding a magic bowl from which a stream of water is ascending.

206.—Incense-burner, Sparrow-hawk on a rock. Fukakusa Faience. Made at *Fushimi, Kyoto, Province of Yamashiro. H. 13 in. Date, 1750.

    The feathers are slightly glazed in black and white.
        (*No.* 235. *Brinkley Collection.*)

207.—Incense-burner, in the form of a Pheasant on a rock. Fukakusa Faience. Made at Fushimi, Kyoto, Province of Yamashiro. H. 9 in.; L. 10 in. Date, 1780.

    The rock and body of the bird are black; wings, green, red and black; space round the eyes, white and red.
        (*No.* 234. *Brinkley Collection.*)

208.—Round Tablet. Sign. Fukakusa Faience. Made at Fushimi, Kyoto, Province of Yamashiro. Diam. 9 in. Date, 1780.

    Design, bird sitting on branch of pine-tree beside a rock: in relief. The bird, tree, and rock, covered with a thin brown glaze.
        (*No.* 236. *Brinkley Collection.*)

---

*Fushimi is a remote suburb of Kyoto.

209.—Incense-burner, in the form of a Pagoda. **Kiyomizu Faience.** Made in Kyoto, Province of Yamashiro. H. 11 in.; Square of base, 5½ in. Date, 1800.

> The roof and basement stones colored dark brown, **the sides** veined to imitate wood. Very delicate workmanship. Mark, *Kakei* (maker's name).
> (*No.* 2450. *Brinkley Collection.*)

210.—Incense-burner, **in the form** of a young Bird, perched on a rock. Kiyomizu Faience. Made in Kyoto, Province of Yamashiro. H. 7⅜ in. Date, 1800.

> Hard gray pâte. Bird covered with a brilliant, deep blue glaze, beak and feet black. Rock, flambé, overrun with blue.

211.—Figure of a Devil raising a lantern. Kiyomizu Faience. Made in Kyoto, Province of Yamashiro. H. 11 in. Date, 1820.

> Unglazed.
> (*No.* 243. *Brinkley Collection.*)

212.—Figure of Buddhist Saint, Daruma. **To simulate a** wood carving. Fukakusa **Faience.** Made at *Fushimi, Kyoto, **Province** of Yamashiro. H. 6 in.; D. 5 in. Date, 1830-40.

> Yellowish red pâte, covered with a dull brown glaze. Beautifully modeled, as though carved from a piece of old wood.
> Signed, *Hokikudo Shujin, tsutsushinde utsushi.* (Made by the Master Hokikudo).
> For description of Daruma, Vide No. 135.

---

*Fushimi is a remote suburb of Kyoto.

213.—**Figure of Kuge Grass-cutter. Fukakusa Pottery.** Made at Fushimi, Kyoto, Province of Yamashiro. H. 7¼ in. L. 9 in. Date, 1840.

White clay, painted in body colors; on the back is an inscription, in relief. *Bunroku san ko-go in gwatsu Koyemon.* (Made on the second month, third, horse, year of Bunroku, (March, 1594,) by Koyemon).

Forgery of Koyemon ware. Proofs: The paste is soft, Koyemon used a hard pâte. The piece is signed; the famous *Ningiyo-ya* (puppet-maker) never signed his productions.

There is a forgery, exactly of this kind, in the South Kensington Museum, London.

214.—**Figure of Yebisu, seated upon a Koi. Modern Kyoto Faience** (*termed Satsuma*). Made in Kyoto, Province of Yamashiro. H. 9½ in. Date, 1870-75.

Dense gray pâte, crackled glaze. Decoration, red, blue, green, black and violet enamels.

215.—**Figure of Hadesu, killing the Korean tiger. Modern Okayama Faience** (*termed Satsuma*). Made in Kyoto, Province of Yamashiro. H. 7⅞ in. Date, 1875-80.

Very fine pâte, close crackle and brilliant glaze, profusely decorated with colored enamels and gold.

In A.D. 545, Kashiwa-déno Omi Hadésu was sent, with his family, as an ambassador from the Japanese Emperor, Kimmei, to Korea. One snowy night Hadésu missed his little daughter from his tent and saw, by the bloody tracks, that she had been carried off by a tiger. He pursued the beast to its lair and, thrusting his hand into its mouth, seized its tongue and drove his sword into its body. (Zenken Kojitsu, Vol. VIII).

CHINESE.

216.—Figure of goddess Kwannon **and** Child attendant. Chinese, Ivory-white Porcelain. H. 9½ in. Date, 1500. (*Hung-che* period).

> Kwannon (Chinese Kwanyin) a Bodhisattva, the daughter of a Chinese king of the Chow dynasty, 696 B.C. She was strangled for disobeying her father, when the latter commanded her to marry against her inclination. When her spirit reached Hades she filled it with joy, whereupon the devil sent her back to earth upon a lotus flower. Finding her father in **prison she fed** him with the flesh of her arms. She is sometimes **worshipped in** Japan as the "Hundred Armed Kwannon."
>
> (*No.* 456. *Brinkley Collection.*)

217.—Figure of Bunsho-sei, (inventor **of writing**), standing on a marine-monster. **Chinese,** White Porcelain. H. 8 in. Date, 1730. (*Yungching* period.)

> A demoniacal figure, resembling the Buddhist Asura. **Holds** in one hand **a box and** in the other **a** brush. He is mounted on an animal which has the head of a dragon, the body and tail of a fish, and wings formed by an expansion of the pectoral fins. The subject is frequently met with in glyptic art. It is probably emblematic of the power and swift dissemination of written thoughts.
>
> (*No.* 457. *Brinkley Collection.*)

218.—Wine-bottle, in the form of a Duck in the act of hissing. Ivory-white Chinese Porcelain. H. 11½ in.; D. 4¼ in. Date, 1723-35. (*Yungching* period).

> Fine pâte and soft ivory glaze, spiritedly modeled.

219.—Figure of Hotei, seated, with a fly-brush (Ch-Hossu. Jap-Futsujin) in his left hand. Chinese White Porcelain. H. 6¼ in.; Base, 6¾ in. Date, 1723-35. (*Yung-ching* period).

> For description of Hotei, Vide No. 179.
> This figure represents the god without his *ho-tei* (cloth-bag).

220.—Incense-burner, in the form of Dog of Fo (*Shishi*). Chinese Stoneware. H. 5 in.; L. 4 in. Date, 1560. (*Kea-tsing*) period.

> Polychromatic. Covered with green glaze in which are metallic spots. On the head and body are nests of concentric circles cut in the pâte.
> For description of *Shishi*, Vide No. 140.
> (*No.* 493. *Brinkley Collection*)

221.—Figure of Sage T'ung Fang-so, holding a peach in his left hand. Chinese Porcelain. H. 7½ in.; Base, 3 in. Date, 1876. (*Kwang-seu* period).

> Polychromatic. Brilliant yellow and flambé crackled glaze.
> (*From the collection of Comte de Semalle, member of the French Legation, at Pekin, from* 1873 *to* 1885.)

222.—Flower-vase, in the form of a Shishi (sky-lion). Chinese Porcelain. H. 9⅛ in. Date, 1736-96. (*Keen-lung* period).

> Decorated with mustard yellow, white, pink, blue, brown and green glazes, finely crackled.
> For description of *Shishi*, Vide No. 140.

223.—Figure of goddess Kwannon, on lotus. Chinese Porcelain. H. 13½ in. Date, 1851-60. (*Han-fung* period).

> Well modeled, and decorated with colored enamels and gold.
> For description of Kwannon, Vide No. 216.

224.—Figure of goddess Kwannon. **Chinese Pottery.**
H. 6¼ in. Date, *unknown*.

Dug up in the Province of Totomi, Japan, in 1840 and purchased by Dr. Louis De Jong of a Japanese collector.

Dense red pâte. Face, body and hands unglazed. Costume covered with heavy yellow, green and lilac glazes.

Very rare and valuable object.

For a description of Kwannon, **Vide No. 216.**

(*From the* **De Jong** *Collection.*)

KOREAN

225.—Flower-vase, in the form of the stump of a **pine-tree**, on the side of which **rests an** incense-burner, in the **form** of a water-jar, with cover. Korean **Porcelain.** H. 8 in.; D. 6¼ in.; Base, 4¼ **in.** Date, 1600-50.

Fine pâte, **bottom** marked with imprint of fabric upon which it was modeled. Covered with a heavy white glaze, decorated with blue under, and red, green and brown enamels, over.

This specimen represents the Korean enameled ware which **was the** prototype of colored Imari.

(*From the De Jong* **Collection.**)

226.—Figure of **Hotei, laughing** and stroking his beard. **Korean Pottery.** H. 9¼ in.; Base, 5¼ in. Date, 1750-1800.

Close-grained hard, gray pâte, covered with a lustrous gray glaze with bluish brown streaks in the folds of the drapery.

(*From the collection of Mr. Pierre L. Jouy.*)

COCHIN-CHINESE.

227.—Incense-box, in the form of an Ox, resting, with a hat on its back. Cochin-Chinese Stoneware. H. 2⅜ in.; L. 3½ in. Date, 1600.

    Covered with a lustrous green glaze, of the same character as the very ancient vase, No. 548 Brinkley collection (No. 367 of this collection) but not as old. Hat, purple. Very curious specimen of Cochin-Chinese ware.
    For description of ox, Vide No. 143.
    (From the De Jong Collection.)

228.—Figure of Hotei. Cochin-Chinese Stoneware. H. 6. in.; Base, 3x2 in. Date, 1600. (H. S.)

    Hard gray pâte, covered in parts with rich, lustrous, iridescent green and yellow glaze. Body unglazed.
    For description of Hotei, Vide No. 179.

229.—Figure of Shishi (sky-lion), on stand. Cochin-Chinese Pottery. H. 8¾ in. Date, 1680-1700.

    Very curious, light pâte, resembling *papier-maché*, covered with a thin green glaze decorated with brown patches.

230.—Figure of a Hare, with a lotus-frond in its mouth. Cochin-Chinese Porcelain. H. 6½ in.; Base, 5⅜x3 in. Date, 1700-50.

    Body covered with incised lines, to represent hair, and decorated with rich green, yellow, and deep purple enamels, over which is a lustrous iridescent glaze.
    In Cochin China, as in Japan, the Hare is the fourth sign of the zodiac.

SECTION SECOND.

CHINESE.

The artistic keramics of China may briefly be classified as follows:

Before Ming. Which includes the famous *K'ienyo* stoneware, celadon stoneware, termed "vases of artificial jade," and early porcelain; the latter being undoubtedly invented during the last part of the *Sung* dynasty—960–1279, A. D. (Probably between 1100–1200).
These wares are of archaic form and decoration, covered with brilliant glazes.

Ming. 1368–1644. When the much prized specimens of monochromatic and polychromatic, and hard and soft paste, colored, **and blue** and white porcelain were produced.
These which, are graceful in form, strong in color and decoration, and covered with exquisite glazes.

Thsing. From 1661 to present time, during which, to end of *Keen-lung*, 1795, occurred *a renaissance culminating in unparalleled perfection.* The most superb specimens of soft and hard paste, of monochromatic, polychromatic, and decorated porcelain, were made during the periods of *Kang-he*, *Yung-ching* and *Keen-lung* and a few during *Kea-King*. Since the beginning of the present century China has produced little that deserves to be classed with the works of her old masters. Brinkley says: "We miss, altogether, the depth and softness of color, fineness of paste, rich, velvety lustre of glaze and brilliancy of enamels that distinguished, as they are infallible evidences, of her Keramic efforts prior to 1800.

The Thsing wares, from Kang-he to Kea-King, are graceful in form, exquisite in color and decoration, and un-rivalled in brillancy and softness of glaze.

This section contains many fine specimens of ivory-white, crackle, monochromatic and polychromatic ware, early examples of blue and white faience, and of porcelain decorated with various colors under and over the glaze. It also illustrates the rise, perfection and decay, of the art of the greatest potters the world has ever known, and proves that they, like their younger brethren, the Japanese, *often copied ancient wares, including the marks and seals, too exactly, without adding a record of the fact;* thus bequeathing to us conundrums exceedingly difficult to solve.

231.—**Bowl, with very small base** and wide rim. **Chinese Porcelain.** H. 2 in.; D. 8 in. Date, 1403-24. (*Yung-lo*).

Ivory white, very thin. On the inside is scroll pattern engraved in the paste.

(*No.* 449. *Brinkley Collection.*)

100

232.—Vase, square in section, with curved sides. Chinese Stoneware. H. 10 in.; Side 7 in. Date, 1470. (*Ching-hwa.*)

    White, rice-colored glaze with bold crackle. Below the rim the crackle assumes the form of concentric circles, over the rest of the surface it runs in all directions. The crackle is of two sizes; the larger, black, and the smaller, brown. Round the lip is a band of key pattern incised.

                 (*No.* 465. *Brinkley Collection.*)

233.—Incense-burner, with three feet. Chinese Porcelain. H. 10 in.; D. 6 in. Date, 1500. (*Hung-che.*)

    Ivory white. Round the body is a band of key pattern and archaic designs incised.

                 (*No.* 452. *Brinkley Collection.*)

234.—Vase. Chinese Porcelain. H. 18¼ in.; D. 8 in. Date, 1670. (*Kang-he.*)

    Plain white. Covered with floral and leaf scrolls, key patterns, etc., in high relief.

                 (*No.* 454. *Brinkley Collection.*)

235.—Vase, square, with tapering neck and base. Chinese Porcelain. H. 8½ in. Date, 1730. (*Yung-ching.*)

    Plain white. Round the rim and shoulder are bands of key pattern and archaic designs in relief. On the sides are circular medallions of wave pattern, also in high relief. Mark of *Yung-ching* period, in relief.

                 (*No.* 458. *Brinkley Collection.*)

236.—**Vase, cylindrical, with tapering base. Chinese Stoneware.** H. 9 in.; D. 4 in. Date, 1730. (*Yung-ching*.)

> Crackled. Cream-colored lustrous glaze, covered with a net-work of pink crackles.
> (*No.* 467. *Brinkley Collection*.)

237.—**Plate. Chinese Porcelain.** H. 1¾ in.; D. 8½ in. Date, 1736-95. (*Keen-lung*.)

> Ivory white, very thin, translucent pâte. Incised decoration, five-clawed dragon and clouds.

238.—**Vase, square above, with rounded body. Chinese Porcelain.** H. 17½ in.; D. 8 in. Date, 1730. (*Yung-ching*.)

> Crackled. Light green glaze with bold and clearly marked crackle. Mark of *Yung-ching* period in blue under the glaze.
> (*No.* 472. *Brinkley Collection*.)

239.—**Cup. Chinese Porcelain.** H. 2 in.; D. 3¼ in. Date, 1750. (*Keen-lung*.)

> Crackled. Covered with a cream white glaze, crackled. Mark, *Ko* (old).
> (*No.* 7173. *Brinkley Collection*.)

240.—**Tea-jar. Chinese Stoneware.** H. 2½ in.; D. 2¼ in. Date, 1650. (*Yung-leih*.)

> Crackled. A rich buff glaze with bold crackle. (From the collection of Ninagawa Noritane.)
> (*No.* 476. *Brinkley Collection*.)

241.—Bon-bon holder. Chinese Stoneware. H. 3½ in.; D. 3 in. Date, 1760. (*Keen-lung.*)

> Crackled. A brownish white glaze with red crackles.
> (*No. 475. Brinkley Collection.*)

242.—Vase, with unglazed handles, in the form of lions' heads. Chinese Stoneware. H. 7 in.; D. 4 in. Date, 1760. (*Keen-lung.*)

> Crackled. A brownish white glaze with red crackles.
> (*No. 478. Brinkley Collection.*)

243.—Vase, with **tapering body and long neck.** Chinese Porcelain. H. 14 in.; D. 7½ in. Date, 1780. (*Keen-lung.*)

> Crackled. A greenish white glaze with bold crackles in black and red.
> (*No. 470. Brinkley Collection.*)

244.—**Vase. Chinese Porcelain.** H. 3½ in.; D. 2¾ in. Date, 1822-50. (*Taou-kwang.*)

> Crackled. **Covered with a cream-colored glaze.** Mark of *Lung-king* period (1567-72). A forgery.

245.—**Bottle, oviform,** with small neck, Raven's wing, **Chinese** Faience. H. 13¼ in.; D. 7½ in.; Base, 4¾ in. Date, 1399-1402. (*Keen-wan.*)

> Very **hard** pâte. Monochromatic. Covered with a thin, mirror-black glaze, charged with violet, intensely iridescent. Known as "Raven's Wing."
>
> Decorated with four *Howo*, in pairs, and with archaic forms of clouds, in brown, in reserve; *i. e.*, the body-glaze is neither over nor under the figures, which are glazed independently.
>
> "Very few examples of this ware have found their way into foreign collections."—*Brinkley.*

246.—**Vase, fluted, with scalloped rim. Chinese, Celadon, Porcelain.** H. 5 in.; D. 3½ in. Date, 1580. (*Wan-leih*.)

> Monochromatic. Covered with a green glaze. On the faces are medallions with coiled dragons, fishes, and clouds in high relief.
> (*No.* 492. *Brinkley Collection.*)

247.—**Incense-burner, silver top. Chinese Porcelain.** H. 3 in.; Width, across handles, 4½ in. Date, 1600. (*Wan-leih*.)

> Monochromatic. A delicate buff glaze with designs in relief.
> (*No.* 506a. *Brinkley Collection.*)

248.—**Vase, mirror-black. Chinese Porcelain.** H. 17⅝ in.; D. 8 in. Date, 1723-35. (*Yung-ching*.)

> Monochromatic. Covered with a lustrous, dark brown glaze, filled with minute yellow specks. (Seen only in a strong light). At a distance the glaze resembles highly polished jet. Fine examples like this are very rare.

249.—**Vase, bottle-shape. Chinese Faience.** H. 14 in.; D. 8¼ in. Date, 1736-95. (*Keen-lung*.)

> Monochromatic. Peacock-blue glaze. Fine, round, fish-roe crackle.

250.—**Vase, semi-globular, with small neck, (*Peach-blow). Chinese Porcelain.** H. 3½ in.; D. 5 in. Date, 1661-1722. (*Kang-he*.)

> Monochromatic. Very fine pâte. Incised decoration, three dragons, in medallions, covered with mottled, peach-blossom glaze.
> Marked, *Ta Thsing, Kang-he, Neen-che.* (Made during the Kanghe period of the great Thsing dynasty.)

---

*Identical in tone, glaze, incised decoration, size and quality, with No. 345 of the Morgan collection.

251.—Vase. Chinese Porcelain. H. 5⅛ in.; D. 2⅞ in. Date, 1661-1722. (*Kang-he.*)

>Monochromatic. Covered with an overfired, pale reddish-gray glaze—termed "ashes of roses;" of the same curious family as "peach-blow," (*i. e.*, an artistic accident, resulting from over-firing).

252.—Bowl, fluted. Chinese Porcelain. H. 3½ in.; D. 7⅙ in. Date, 1680. (*Kang-he.*)

>Monochromatic. Covered with an exceedingly lustrous, light lilac glaze flecked with white.
>(*No.* 517. *Brinkley Collection.*)

253.—Bowl and saucer. Chinese Porcelain. H. 2¼ in.; D. of bowl, 4½ in.; D. of saucer, 5½ in. Date, 1700. (*Kang-he.*)

>Monochromatic. **Covered with a lustrous indigo glaze** having a tinge of purple.
>(*No.* 528. *Brinkley Collection.*)

254.—Low, flat bottle, semi-globular shape, ormolu neck. **Chinese** Porcelain. H. without stand, 3½ in.; with stand, 4 in.; D. 5 in. Date, 1661-1722. (*Kang-he.*)

>Monochromatic. Verdigris green glaze, with cloudings and mottles of red. Three medallions or crests incised under the glaze. Mark, *Ta Thsing, Kang-he, Nien-che.*
>(*No.* **300**. *Morgan Collection.*)

255.—Plate. Chinese Porcelain. H. 1½ in.; D. 7½ in. Date, 1750. (*Keen-lung.*)

>Monochromatic. Covered with a peach-blossom-red glaze. Mark of *Shunti* period (1426-1436). A forgery.
>(*No.* 538. *Brinkley Collection.*)

256.—**Vase, melon-shape,** tapering neck, silver top. Chinese Faience. H. 8¾ in.; D. 7 in. Date, 1736-95. (*Keen-lung.*)

> Monochromatic. Light mustard yellow. Compound crackle.

257.—**Water-jar, in the form of a basket covered with cash.** Chinese, Celadon Porcelain. H. 4 in.; D. 6½ in. Date, 1796-1821. (*Kea-king.*)

> Monochromatic. Covered with a green glaze. Marked, *Kea-king neen-che* (period of Kea-king, Ta Th'sing dynasty).

257*a*.—**Vase, oviform, with spreading neck, elephant-head handles.** Chinese, sea-green Celadon Porcelain. H. 11⅛ in.; D. 8¾ in. Date, 1736-95. (*Keen-lung.*)

> Monochromatic. Archaic form, copied from metal-work. Very clear, brilliant glaze.

257*b*.—**Vase, oviform, with narrow neck.** Chinese, Celadon, Stoneware. H. 4¾ in.; D. 3⅛ in. Date, 1426-35. (*Seuen-te.*)

> Monochromatic. Upper section decorated with scrolls in semi-relief; lower with lanceolated leaves. Covered with rich, green glaze.

258.—**Pen (brush) washer.** Chinese Stoneware. H. ½ in.; D. 2¼ in. Date, 1800. (*Kea-king.*)

> Monochromatic. Covered with a dark apple-green glaze finely crackled. Inside is a crab in high relief and covered with a greenish black glaze.
> (*No.* 542. *Brinkley Collection.*)

259.—Vase, bottle-shape. Chinese Porcelain. H. 5 in. D. 3½ in. Date, 1851-60. (*Han-fung.*)

    Monochromatic. Pea green glaze, **crackled in patches.**

260.—Cup. Chinese, Kien-yo Stoneware, with **silver rim.** H. 2½ in.; D. 5 in. Date, 1125.

    Polychromatic. Lustrous black glaze, having purple and blue tints and regulary marked fine metallic lines. (From the collection of Ninagawa Noritane.) Stand of black and gold lacquer.

        (*No.* 648. *Brinkley Collection.*)

261.—Bowl. Chinese Porcelain. H. 2¾ in.; D. 5 in. Date, 1500. (*Hung-che.*)

    Polychromatic. A rich brown, with storks and lotus plants, in white, in slight relief.

        (*No.* 623. *Brinkley Collection.*)

262.—Tea-jar. Chinese Pottery. H. 2 in.; D. 1¾ in. Date, 1600. (*Wan-leih.*)

    Polychromatic. **A lustrous brown glaze,** flecked with blue.

        (*No.* 590. *Brinkley Collection.*)

263.—Dish, in form of three pine leaves, (Qy. outline of a snow-laden branch of pine.) Chinese Stoneware. H. 1¾ in.; L. 8½ in.; B. 4 in. Date, 1600. (*Wan-leih.*)

    Polychromatic. **Pink glaze, flecked** with blue and white.

        (*No.* 613. *Brinkley Collection.*)

264.—Vase, rectangular in section. Chinese Stoneware. H. 6 in.; Sides, 3½x3 in. Date, 1650. (*Yung-leih.*)

    Polychromatic. Dark red glaze, flecked with purple.

        (*No.* 560. *Brinkley Collection.*)

265.—**Vase.** Chinese Stoneware. H. 11 in.; D. 4 in. Date, 1650. (*Yung-leih.*)

> Polychromatic. A purplish glaze, beautifully flecked with blue and white.
> (*No. 573. Brinkley Collection.*)

266.—**Vase, egg-shaped.** Chinese Stoneware. H. 9½ in.; D. 6¼ in. Date, 1680. (*Kang-he.*)

> Polychromatic. Dark brown, flecked and spotted with blue.
> (*No. 569. Brinkley Collection.*)

267.—**Vase, with trumpet-shaped neck.** Chinese Porcelain. H. 13½ in.; D. 9 in. Date, 1680. (*Kang-he.*)

> Polychromatic. An iron-red glaze, covered with very fine metallic spots.
> (*No. 633. Brinkley Collection.*)

268.—**Vase, with swelling body and tapering neck and base.** Chinese Porcelain. H. 7½ in.; D. 3 in. Date, 1700. (*Kang-he.*)

> Polychromatic. A dead-leaf glaze, with dark metallic spots.
> (*No. 634. Brinkley Collection.*)

269.—**Vase.** Chinese Porcelain. H. 4 in.; D. 1¾ in. Date, 1700. (*Kang-he.*)

> Polychromatic. A lustrous red glaze, with fine metallic spots.
> (*No. 638. Brinkley Collection.*)

270.—**Tea-jar.** Chinese Porcelain. H. 4½ in.; D. 3½ in. Date, 1700. (*Kang-he.*)

> Polychromatic. A lustrous iron-rust glaze, with minute, metallic spots.

271.—Cup. Chinese Porcelain. H. 2 in.; D. 3½ in. Date, 1700. (*Kang-he*.)

> Polychromatic. An exceedingly rich blue *soufflé* glaze.
> (*No.* 645. *Brinkley* Collection.)

272.—Tea-pot. Chinese Stoneware. H. 3½ in.; Width, 5 in. Date, 1720. (*Kang-he*.)

> Polychromatic. Pâte as light as cork. The body is unglazed, but is divided by ribs of white glaze into six panels, containing landscapes in green and red **enamels on a groundwork of diapers**. All the designs **are in relief.**
> (*No.* 623. *Brinkley* Collection.)

273.—Sweetmeat-bowl. Chinese Porcelain. H. 3 in.; D. top, 9 in.; Base, 3⅛ in. Date, 1723-35. (*Yung-ching*.)

> Polychromatic. Irregularly covered with a blood-red splash. Pale green glaze.

274.—Vase. Chinese Stoneware. Silver top. H. 13 in.; D. 7½ in. Date, 1739. (*Keen-lung*.)

> Polychromatic. A rich, variegated glaze of eel's-blood red, greenish brown, blue, and pinkish white, run together with considerable regularity.
> (*No.* 614. *Brinkley Collection.*)

275.—Vase (snuff-bottle). **Chinese** Porcelain. H. 2¼ in.; D. 1¾ **in.** Date, 1750. (*Keen-lung*.)

> Polychromatic. Covered with an olive green glaze in which are mixed speckles of yellow. Mark of *Keen-lung* period.
> (*No.* 555. *Brinkley Collection.*)

276.—**Vase. Chinese Stoneware.** H. 7 in.; D. 3 in. Date, 1750. (*Keen-lung.*)

    Polychromatic. A lustrous glaze of blue, green white, metallic red, and claret-colored tints.
(*No.* 578. *Brinkley Collection.*)

277.—**Brush-washer. Chinese Pottery.** H. 2 in.; L. 2 in. Date, 1750. (*Keen-lung.*)

    Polychromatic. A soft lustrous green glaze run over a buff glaze. The outside is fluted, the flutes showing buff-color through the glaze.
(*No.* 595. *Brinkley Collection.*)

278.—**Vase. Chinese Porcelain.** H. 15 in.; D. 9 in. Date, 1760. (*Keen-lung.*)

    Polychromatic. A light mauve glaze, with designs in slight relief appearing white under the glaze.
(*No.* 620. *Brinkley Collection.*)

279.—**Vase, with lion-head handles. Chinese Stoneware.** H. 14 in.; D. 10 in. Date, 1780. (*Keen-lung.*)

    Polychromatic. A lustrous glaze of blue, green, and brown tints. Mark, *Koh Ming Tsiang-chi.* (Made by Koh Ming Tsiang). The mark is forged.
(*No.* 565. *Brinkley Collection.*)

280.—**Vase, bulb-shaped, with narrow, tapering neck. Chinese Faience.** H. 7¾ in.; D. 5 in. Base, 2¼ in. Date, 1796-1821. (*Taou-kwang.*)

    Polychromatic. Covered with a blood-red glaze, flambé, with purple, gray and black.

281.—**Snuff-bottle. Chinese Porcelain.** H. 2¼ in.; D. 1½ in. Date, 1800. (*Kea-king*.)

> Polychromatic. A variegated glaze of indigo and green.
> (*No.* 603. *Brinkley Collection.*)

282.—**Vase. Chinese Stoneware.** H. 7½ in.; D. 5½ in. Date, 1800. (*Kea-king*.)

> Polychromatic. The vase has eight vertical flutes, down which run lines of rich blue glaze with white borders. Between the flutes the glaze is red, flecked with blue. Mark of the period, *Kea-king*.
> (*No.* 615. *Brinkley Collection.*)

283.—**Incense-box. Chinese Porcelain.** H. 1½ in.; D. 3 in. Date, 1800. (*Kea-king*.)

> Polychromatic. A mustard-yellow glaze. Round the base is a band of leaves and a key pattern in high relief. On the top is the character *Ju* (congratulation) in blue, in relief, and round it is a triple band of key pattern with archaic designs in green, blue and purple, in relief. Mark of *Kea-king* period.
> (*No.* 625. *Brinkley Collection.*)

284.—**Vase. Chinese Stoneware.** H. 14 in.; D. 7 in. Date, 1800. (*Kea-king*.)

> Polychromatic. A rich brown glaze, flecked with blue and white.
> (*No.* 647*a*. *Brinkley Collection.*)

285.—**Vase, with sceptre-shaped handles. Chinese Porcelain.** H. 8¼ in.; D. 5½ in. Date, 1822-50. (*Taou-kwang*.)

> Polychromatic. Mustard yellow, over which is a floral design in colored enamels. Opalescent glaze.

286.—**Vase, with swelling body and long narrow neck.** Chinese Stoneware. H. 8 in.; D. 4¼ in. Date, 1820. (*Kea-king.*)

> Polychromatic. Blood-red glaze, flecked with black and tinged with purple at the neck.
> (*No.* 562. *Brinkley Collection.*)

287.—**Vase. Chinese Faience.** H. 6 in.; D. 2½ in. Date, 1830. (*Taou-kwang.*)

> Polychromatic. Turquoise blue glaze, flecked with purple.
> (*No.* 597. *Brinkley Collection.*)

288.—**Plate. Chinese Porcelain.** H. 2½ in.; D. 16½ in. Date, 1830. (*Taou-kwang.*)

> Polychromatic. A slate-blue glaze, with a design of three *shishi*, a ball, and streamers in lilac and black, in relief.
> (*No.* 644. *Brinkley Collection.*)

289.—**Vase, oviform, with dragon coiled about neck and upper section.** Chinese Porcelain. H. 5⅜ in.; D. 3¼ in. Date, 1822-50. (*Taou-kwang.*)

> Polychromatic. Body covered with a lavender glaze. Dragon, mauve-colored, decorated with darker spots. Mark, *Ta Th'sing Taou-kwang Neen-che.*

290.—**Dish. Chinese, Blue and White Stoneware.** H. 3¼ in.; D. 10½ in. Date, 951-59. (*Chow* dynasty).

> Decorated with archaic designs, in blue, covered with a thick, semi-opaque glaze.
> (Some specimens resembling this, treasured in Japan, are said to be fifteen hundred years old.)
> (*From the De Jong Collection.*)

291. **Fire-holder.** Chinese, Blue and **White Porcelain.** H. 2½ in.; D. 4½ in. Date, 1200. (During *Sung* dynasty):

A yellowish white glaze, with a roughly executed design, in dark blue, of a castle and various circles, spirals, etc., under the glaze. This specimen shows the earliest attempts of the Chinese to produce porcelain. (From the collection of Ninagawa Noritane.)

(*No.* 657. *Brinkley Collection.*)

292.—**Dish.** Chinese, **Blue and White Porcelain.** H. 3¼ in.; D. 15 in. Date, 1399-1402. (*Keentsun*).

Fine pâte. Decorated with archaic forms in blue under a heavy glaze such as, before the discovery of feldspathic glaze, was used on pottery and stoneware.

An early specimen of true, Chinese porcelain.

(*From the De Jong Collection.*)

293.—Bowl. **Chinese, Blue and White Porcelain.** H. 3 in.; D. 8½ in. Date, 1426-36. (*Seuen-te*).

Covered inside and outside with branches of trees and shrubs, under the glaze. Mark of *Seuen-te* period to which it belongs. (From the collection of Ninagawa Noritane.)

(*No.* 660. *Brinkley Collection.*)

294.—Bowl. Chinese, Blue **and** White Porcelain. H. 3 in.; D. 8 in. Date, 1650. (*Yung-leih*).

The inside plain; the outside decorated with figure subjects, under the glaze. Mark, *Seuen-te* period (1426). A forgery.

(*No.* 674. *Brinkley Collection.*)

295.—Bowl. Chinese, Blue and White Porcelain. H. 4 in.; D. 8 in. Date, 1660. (*Yung-leih*).

> On the bottom, inside, a *Kirin*. Outside, children at play, houses, trees, etc., in very dark blue, under the glaze.
> (*No. 682. Brinkley Collection.*)

296.—Bowl. Chinese, Blue and White Porcelain. H. 4 in.; D. 8 in. Date, 1680. (*Kang-he*).

> Inside plain. Outside a delicately executed design of children at play, trees and flowers, under the glaze.
> (*No. 681. Brinkley Collection.*)

297.—Vase, cylindrical. Chinese, Blue and White Porcelain. H. 10½ in.; D. 3½ in. Date, 1680. (*Kang-he*).

> Decoration, figure subjects, trees, rocks, etc. Round the shoulders and base are bands of incised diapers, under the glaze.
> (*No. 689. Brinkley Collection.*)

298.—Wine-bottle, cylindrical, with narrow neck. Chinese, Blue and White Porcelain. H. 9 in.; D. 3 in. Date, 1700. (*Kang-he*).

> Body divided by horizontal lines into four bands of decoration; lowest vine pattern in white on blue ground; the second, diapers and flowers; the third, landscapes; and the fourth diapers. The neck decorated inside with spiral bands of blue.
> This piece is a Chinese imitation of the famous Japanese Shonzui-ware.
> (*No. 5. Brinkley Collection.*)

299.—Cup. Chinese, Blue and White Porcelain. H
2.; D. 2⅝ in. Date, 1700. (*Kang-he*)

Thin pâte, decorated with cocks, hens, chickens, and floral designs in blue under the glaze. Mark, *Hi-tso ki-gwin chi hiu*. (Precious and rare toy *for use* at sunrise.)
(*No.* 717ᵃ *Brinkley Collection.*)

300.—Incense-box, in the shape of an egg-plant. Chinese, Blue and White Porcelain. H. 1¼ in.; L. 2¼ in. Date, 1736-95. (*Keen-lung*).

Decoration, a diaper of deep blue bands, among which are white plum petals. Mark, *Keen-lung*.
(*No.* 711. *Brinkley Collection.*)

301.—Jar, with lid. **Chinese, Blue and White Porcelain.** H. 9¼ in.; D. 8 in. Date, 1736-95. (*Keen-lung*).

Hawthorne pattern (plum) in deep blue under glaze.

302.—Vase. **Chinese, Blue and White Porcelain.** H. 10 in.; D. 4¾ in. Date, 1796-1821. (*Kea-king*).

Conventional decoration, in starch blue, under a very soft glaze.

303.—Vase, archaic shape. Chinese, Blue and White Soft Paste. H. 21½ in.; D. 8¾ in. Date, 1723-35. (*Yung-ching*).

Very light, soft pâte. Milk white glaze. Decoration, *shishi* (sky-lion) feeding its young, under a *lychee* tree, bamboo trees and bats (emblems of longevity) in superb, deep blue.

The surface is pitted like the rind of an orange, and has vertical crackles.
(*From the Arbuthnot Collection.*)

304.—Vase, cylindrical, with flaring neck and elephant-head handles. Chinese Porcelain. H. 8¼ in.; D. 4¾ in. Date, 1661-1721. (*Kang-he*).

> Decoration, *Howo* and *Botan*, in blue and sepia, under the glaze. Mark of *Ching-hwa* period (1465-87.) A forgery.

305.—Plate. Chinese Porcelain. Various colors under the glaze. H. 1½ in.; D. 6½ in. Date, 1700. (*Kang-he*).

> Round the edge, outside, are eight Genii riding upon fishes, leaves, fabulous animals, etc., among conventional waves. The figures are blue; the waves red. On the bottom, inside, are figures of Fuku-roku-jin and stag, in blue, among red waves.
> Mark, *Yok-hian Su-ok*. (Hall of diligent painting.)
> (*No.* 719. *Brinkley Collection.*)

306.—Vase, bottle-shape. Chinese Porcelain. Various colors under the glaze. H. 14⅛ in.; D. 9 in. Date, 1723-36. (*Yung-ching*).

> Decorated with a four clawed dragon, in sepia and incised wave pattern, under the glaze.
> Mark of *Ching-hwa* period (1465-87), but true date as above.

307.—Vase. Chinese Porcelain. Various colors under the glaze. H. 3½ in.; D. 1½ in. Date, 1750. (*Keen-lung*).

> Curiously marbled with red and blue.
> (*No.* 721. *Brinkley Collection.*)

308.—**Brush-holder, cylindrical.** Porcelain. Various colors under the glaze. H. 4½ in.; D. 2⅔ in. Date, 1736-95. (*Keen-lung*).

    Decoration, a dragon, clouds, and flames in light green. The design is incised. Mark, and date, *Keen-lung*.

    (*No.* 726. *Brinkley Collection*.)

309.—**Vase.** Chinese Porcelain. Various colors under the glaze. H. 9 in.; D. 3½ in. Date, 1800. (*Kea-king*).

    A mustard-yellow glaze, with a design of flowers **and leaves** in dark brown.

    (*No.* 725. *Brinkley Collection*.)

310.—**Vase.** Chinese Porcelain. **Various colors under the** glaze. H. 18½ in.; D. 8 in. Date, 1820. (*Kea-king*).

    Decorated with horses, trees, and rocks in blue, liver-color and black.

    (*No.* 724. *Brinkley Collection*.)

311.—**Plate.** Chinese Porcelain. Various colors. H. 4 in.; D. 15 in. Date, 1450. (*King-tae*).

    In the centre is a fabulous monster among hills and shrubs. Round the rim are bands of diaper with medallions containing floral subjects, birds, etc. Colors, red and green over, and blue under the glaze. This ware is known in Japan as *Gosu aka-ye*, and is said to represent the earliest enameled porcelain produced in China.

    (*No.* 729. *Brinkley Collection*.)

312.—**Vase, oviform, with silver rim. Black Hawthorne, Chinese Porcelain.** H. 17⅛ in.; D. 8½ in.; Base, 6⅛ in. Date, 1465-87. (*Ching-hwa*).

> Decoration, plum (so-called Hawthorne) blossoms and branches, rocks and birds in brilliant green, purple and yellow enamels, white blossoms in reserve. Body a jet-black enamel, charged upon a grass green. No mark.
> (*From the Arbuthnot Collection.*)

313.—**Jar, with silver rim. Chinese Porcelain. Various colors.** H. 6½ in.; D. 6 in. Date, 1550. (*Kea-tsing*.)

> Round the shoulder is a band of green with a floral scroll in red and white. The body is red, with flowers and leaves in white and green.
> (*No.* 730. *Brinkley Collection.*)

314.—**Incense-burner, square in section, with lion (shishi) and ball on top. Chinese Porcelain. Various colors.** H. 6¾ in.; Square, 4¼ x 4¼ in. Date, 1600. (*Wan-leih*).

> The base is covered with a floral scroll in green and purple. On the sides are figure subjects in green, red and yellow under, and blue over the glaze. The lion is green and gold. Mark (on top rim) of *Ching-hwa* period (1465). A forgery.
> (*No.* 736. *Brinkley Collection.*)

315.—**Bowl. Chinese Porcelain. Various colors.** Black and gold lacquer stand. H. 2½ in.; D. 6 in. Date, 1640. (*Tsung-ching*).

> Decorated inside with storks, grasses, and conventional trees in rich blue, under the glaze. Round the outside of rim is a band of diaper in blue, and on the body are figures in red, green, and yellow enamels, over, separated by blue scrolls, under the glaze. Mark of *Kea-tsing* period (1522). A forgery.
> (*No.* 738. *Brinkley Collection.*)

316.—**Bowl.** Chinese Porcelain. **Various colors.** H.
4 in.; D. 8 in. Date, 1736-95. (*Keen-lung*).

Round the base and rim are bands of key pattern in blue. The body is covered with a wave diaper in red and white, among which are fabulous monsters in blue. Mark, **and date,** K'een-lung period.

(*No. 754. Brinkley Collection.*)

317.—**Bowl.** Chinese Porcelain. Various colors. H.
4 in.; D. 9 in. Date, 1740. (*Keen-lung*).

Decoration, dragons in red with clouds and flames over, and a band of diaper in blue, under the glaze.

(*No. 751. Brinkley Collection.*)

318.—**Cup.** Chinese Porcelain. Enamel colors **over** the glaze. H. 1¾ in.; D. 3¼ in. Date, 1750. (*Keen-lung*).

Decorated with dragons and floral scrolls in red, green, and yellow. Mark of *Wan-leih* period (1573). A forgery.

(*No. 7174. Brinkley Collection.*)

319.—**Cup.** Chinese Porcelain. Various colors. Black and gold lacquer stand. H. 2½ in.; D. 4¼ in. Date, 1780. (*Keen-lung*).

Thin porcelain, with delicately executed dragons in red **over,** and blue under the glaze, and round the rim a band of archaic **symbols.** Mark of *Ching-hwa* period (1465). A forgery.

(*No. 747. Brinkley Collection.*)

320.—**Cup.** Chinese Porcelain. Various **colors.** Gold lacquer stand. H. 2 in.; D. 4½ in. **Date,** 1830. (*Taou-kwang*).

Decoration, lotus leaves and flowers in blue under, and green, pink and gold over the glaze. The petals of the flowers are pierced and filled in with green glaze. Mark of K'een-*lung* period (1736). A forgery.

(*No. 746. Brinkley Collection.*)

321.—Cup. Chinese Porcelain. Various colors. H. 1 in.; D. 2¾ in. Date, 1850. (*Taou-kwang*).

> Decorated with rocks, flowers, cocks, hens, and chickens, in red, blue, yellow, green and gold.
>
> (*No.* 744.   *Brinkley Collection*.)

322.—Vase, square in section, with tapering base and neck. Chinese Porcelain. Various colors. H. 15¼ in.; Side, 6 in. Date, 1860. (*Han-fung*).

> On each side is a figure, delicately executed in blue, green, red, and yellow enamels. On the shoulders are various verses of poetry, and on the neck, circular medallions and half opened scrolls, also containing characters. The surface of the glaze is slightly indented.
>
> (*No.* 743   *Brinkley Collection*.)

323.—Vase, cylindrical form, tapering towards base. Rounded Shoulders and small neck. Chinese, Semi Egg-shell Porcelain. Various colors. H. 9 in.; D. 4 in. Date, 1861-75. (*Thung-she*).

> Decoration, floral designs in red, blue and gold. River scenes in reserved spaces.

324.—Vase, flat beaker-shaped, with scroll handles. Chinese Porcelain. Various colors. H. 8 in.; D. 3½ in. Date, 1861-75. (*Thung-she*).

> Covered with turquoise blue jewel-points. Landscapes, figures and flowers, in reserved spaces. Mark of *Keen-lung* period (1736-95).
>
> (*No.* 422.   *Morgan Collection*.)

325.—Vase, square in section, tapering **downwards.**
Square, flange top. Chinese **Porcelain.**
Various colors. H. 12 in.; Square, 3¾ in.;
Base, 2¼ in. Date, 1876. (*Kwang-seu*).

    Decorated, in reserved panels, with flowers in colored enamels, over the glaze. Neck, conventional bands with reserved spaces containing representations of "The Precious Objects" and floral designs.

326.—Vase, flattened oviform, with handles and **cover.** Chinese Porcelain. Various colors.
H. 9 in.: D. 4¼ in. Date, 1876. (*Kwang-seu*).

    Decorated with green enamel covered with red flowers. Two reserved spaces containing **scenes.**

327.—**Brush-holder, cylindrical.** Chinese Porcelain. **Various colors.** H. 5¼ in.; D. 5 in. Date, 1876. (*Kwang-seu*).

    Coral-red glaze with conventional, floral designs in colored enamels.

328.—**Plate.** Chinese Porcelain. Rose-back. H. 1$\frac{5}{14}$ in.; D. 7¼ in. Date, 1876. (*Kwang-seu*).

    Semi egg-shell, decorated inside with three cocks, **and flowers,** in brilliant, colored enamels.

329.—**Bowl and cover.** Chinese **Porcelain.** Various colors. H. 5 in.; D. 8½ in. Date, 1876-80. (*Kwang-seu*).

    Semi egg-shell. Celadon glaze, decorated with flowers in colored enamels. Gilt edge. Mark of *Kwang-seu* period. Reign of present Emperor, the regency of which began in 1876. (*No.* 483. *Morgan Collection.*) Entered by mistake as "Mark of the *Kang-he* period, (1661-1722)."

330.—**Water-vessel**, square in section, with bamboo edges, spout and handle. Chinese, Boccaro, Faience. H. 5 in., Side, 3 in. Date, 1780. (*Keen-lung*).

On the sides are circles of bamboo with the *Swastika* (symbol of Buddha's heart and of ten thousand years), inside in relief.

(*No.* 777. *Brinkley Collection.*)

SECTION THIRD.

KOREAN.

Before Chöson was open to foreigners, in 1883, the Keramic arts of that mysterious country were only known to us by the specimens, treasured by Japanese Archæologists as prototypes of the wares of their own country. These by no means proved the assertion made by foreigners who had never visited China, that "Korea was the source of Japanese art"; an opinion shared by many highly educated Japanese.

The unique collection of Korean mortuary pottery and of modern domestic ware, made by Mr. Pierre L. Jouy during a three years' residence in various parts of the country, and specimens recently procured from Söul, show, that while the ancient Koreans made "pottery infants" strongly resembling those attributed to the autochthons of Japan, their modern productions are far inferior to those of their Eastern neighbors.

It is probably true that, as far back as the beginning of the Christian era, the Koreans instructed the then more barbarous Japanese in the potter's art, and it is also undeniable that, during the 14th and 15th centuries, they made exquisite ivory-white porcelain (Nos. 359 and 366) in no way inferior to the famous ware of China; though none of these facts prove the assertion to which I have referred.

An examination of the fragments of ancient wares, found in India, China, Korea and Japan, will convince the student, that *all the forms and decorative motives employed by those nations had a common origin among a race, every other trace of which had been obliterated by the hand of Time*. No one who, has visited those countries and seen the relics of archaic pottery found in all of them, will deny that the origin of Japanese art lay in the far East and that while it acquired its strength and beauty from Brahmanism and Buddhism, and something of the local color of India and China, it underwent some change in traveling the road of Korea, through which it undoubtedly entered Japan. How far this applies to the art of working in metals, many of the decorations of which are said, by Japanese, to be of purely Korean origin, has no bearing upon the question of Keramics, there being little doubt that, many centuries ago, the Koreans were masters of the art of bronze-casting, etc., and probably improved upon the methods of their teachers; which cannot be said of their potters.

This collection contains specimens that have been treasured by Japanese connoisseurs (Nos. 350 to 363) and of modern pottery (Nos. 364 and 365) including an example of the "new ware" (No. 366a) manufactured by "experts who, in 1881-2, were sent to Japan, to learn the art of making porcelain." I have grouped this, with the beautiful ivory-white vase (No. 366) made during the 15th century, in order to illustrate the present awful degeneration of the potters' art in "The Land of the Morning Calm."

350.—Bowl, irregular shape. Korean Pottery. H. 2½ in.; D. 5 in. Date, 800-900.

Very light paste covered with a yellowish mottled glaze. An exceedingly curious, archaic specimen.
(*From the De Jong Collection.*)

351.—Shallow bowl. Korean Pottery. H. 1½ in.; D. 5⅞ in. Date, 800-900.

Soft paste covered with a yellowish crackled glaze on upper section inside and out, as though dipped. Exceedingly curious, archaic specimen.
(*From the De Jong Collection.*)

352.—Vase, with bulbous base and trumpet shape neck, curious handles. Korean Faience. H. 9 in.; D. 10 in. Date, 900-1000.

Very hard gray pâte overrun with an exceedingly curious brown glaze, the lower portion having a deep, iridescent, raven's wing, bluish tone.

An exceedingly rare specimen of Korean faience, anterior to Ko-Karatsu ware.

353.—Bowl. Korean Stoneware. H. 2 in.; D. 5¾ in. Date, 1100.

Heavy, hard gray pâte, covered with a slate-colored glaze incised with lines and archaic designs, inside and out, filled with white clay.

Excellent example of the ancient Korean ware from which old Karatsu, Yatsushiro, and other Japanese wares were modeled.
(*From the De Jong Collection.*)

354.—Vase, tapering base, swelling body, and cup-shaped neck. Korean Faience. H 8⅞ in.; D. 5 in. Date, 1100.

Hard gray pâte, partly overrun with a brilliant, heavy, white, crackled, enamel glaze, not extending to base, forming irregular points.
Curious and rare specimen of ancient Korean ivory white.

(*From the De Jong Collection.*)

355.—Stirrup-cup, in the form of **a rice-mortar**. Korean Faience. H. 4¼ in.; D. 5 in. Date, 1200.

Soft, cream-colored glaze, in which are four forms of crackle.

(*From the De Jong Collection.*)

356.—**Vase, with narrow base and swelling body. Korean Stoneware.** H. 13 in.; D. 12 in. Date, 1300.

Cream-colored glaze finely crackled. **Round** the base and shoulder are lines and a band of **diaper**. **On** the sides are three large medallions bordered by broad black lines. One medallion contains the figure of an old man seated; behind him is a fir tree with a gourd hanging from its branches; before him, conventional waves and a design intended to represent the constellation of *ursa major* (*Sh'chyano hoshi*). The second medallion contains a stork flying down towards reeds and lotus plants. The third, an open lily surrounded by leaves. All the decoration is in very dark brown, and the inside is covered with a glaze of that color.

(*No. 779. Brinkley Collection.*)

357.—Vase, with narrow base and swelling body. Korean Stoneware. H. 11½ in.; D. 12 in. Date, 1300.

>Covered inside and outside with a cream-colored glaze. Round the neck are two bands of floral scroll in red and green enamels. Round the base, a band of conventional leaves. Round the body are three large medallions. In one is a man seated on a fish swimming in green waves: in the distance are mountains and a castle. In another are two figures, with trees, a hill, etc., in green and red. In the third, the same two figures in different positions, with flowers, trees, etc., in green and red. [This is a very remarkable specimen. Korean ware decorated with colored enamels is exceedingly rare, so much so, indeed, that its very existence has been doubted. The present specimen has been preserved in the province of Kaga since 1598.]
>(*No.* 780. *Brinkley Collection.*)

358.—Bowl, of graceful form. Korean Stoneware. H. 4 in.; D. 5⅛ in. Date, 1400.

>Very heavy stoneware, slightly glazed inside and on upper outer section.
>(*From the De Jong Collection.*)

359.—Hexagonal box. Korean, Ivory-white Porcelain. H. 2 in.; D. 3 ¼ in. Date, 1450.

>Soft ivory-white glaze. On the top is a branch of the tree peony in high relief. Round this is a band of floral scroll, and on the side are plum blossoms and sprays, in relief.
>(*No.* 796. *Brinkley Collection.*)

360.—Bowl, of graceful form, intended to represent an open lotus flower. Korean Stoneware. H. 3 in.; D. 6⅜ in. Date, 1500.

>Hard, gray pâte, incised outside, to represent the outlines of a lotus flower, covered with a heavy, sage-color, crackled glaze.
>(*From the De Jong Collection.*)

361.—Incense-box, lozenge-shaped, with one indentation. Korean Stoneware. H. 1 in.; D. 2½ x 1¾ in. Date, 1550.

Heavy pâte, covered with a reddish-buff glaze. On the top is a cow in relief partially covered with a brownish green glaze.

(No. 782. Brinkley Collection.)

362.—Bowl. Korean **Pottery.** H. 3¼ in.; D. 5¾ in. Date, 1550.

Yellowish gray pâte, covered with heavy cream-colored glaze.

(From the De Jong Collection.)

363.—Bowl, of irregular square form. Korean Faience. H. 3¼ in.; D. 4⅝ in. Date, 1580-90.

Heavy, close pâte, incised decoration, storks and flowers, between horizontal lines, filled with white clay, slightly decorated with black. Inside and upper outer section covered with a heavy cream-color glaze overrun with a thinner glaze.

A specimen of the encaustic faience from which Yatsushiro ware was copied.

(From the De Jong Collection.)

364.—Bowl. Korean **Stoneware.** H. 2⅝ in.; D. 6⅝ in. Date, 1800-50.

Hard, gray pâte, covered with an exceedingly beautiful soft celadon, crazed glaze.

Procured in Sôul, in 1886, by a Japanese dealer.

365.—Bowl. Korean **Pottery.** H. 2¾ in.; D. 7½ in. Date, 1850-80.

Soft, coarse white pâte, inside decorated with floral designs in semi-relief. The entire body covered with a heavy, dull celadon glaze.

Excellent specimen of Korean pottery of present century, as contrasting with the old, for which it is often mistaken.

Procured in Sôul, in 1886, by a Japanese dealer.

366.—Vase, cylindrical, with slightly tapering base and lion-head handles. Korean, Ivory-white Porcelain. H. 12⅛ in.; D. 6 in. Date, 1450.

Soft, ivory-white glaze with a pinkish tinge.

366a.—Vase, in conventional form of an inverted and an open lotus flower. Korean Porcelain. H. 3⅝ in.; D. 3 in. Date, 1883.

Pâte, rough and poorly finished showing a lack of technique. Decoration, coarsely executed floral scrolls, with blossoms, in yellow, green and pink enamels, badly fired. Band of common (foreign) imitation gold about center.

This example is particularly interesting on account of its illustrating the present degenerated state of keramics in Korea.

In 1881-2 the King of Korea sent experts to Japan "to learn the art of making porcelain," from which it would appear it had fallen into desuetude. Upon their return they established a kiln at Söul, where this specimen was manufactured. It was presented to its late owner as "a sample of the new ware."

(*From the Collection of Mr. Pierre L. Jouy.*)

SECTION FOURTH.

COCHIN-CHINESE.

"Japanese connoisseurs believe that, from very ancient times, the keramists of the Cochin-Chinese peninsula sent consignments of pottery to Japan, and the intercourse of the two nations was sufficiently intimate to bear out this tradition.

"This ware was known as *Kochi-yaki* and was one of the foreign productions copied by the famous Kyoto potter, *Kiya-sahei Mokubei.*"—*Brinkley.*

367.—Vase, globular, with tapering base. **Cochin-Chinese Stoneware.** H. 9 in.; D. 7 in. Date, 900.

> Monochromatic. Heavy pâte, covered with a dark green glaze. (From the collection of Ninagawa Noritane.) The clay and glaze of this piece are identical with those of the tiles brought over from Cochin-China in the ninth century for the purpose of roofing a Japanese temple near Kyoto.
>
> (*No. 548. Brinkley Collection.*)

SECTION FIFTH.

BRIC-A-BRAC.

400.—**Group of Buddhistic figures, in ivory, mounted upon a curious base, of jinko-root, and a red-wood stand. Japanese.** Carved in Tokyo. H. 24 in.; L. 24 in. Date, 1876.

> The central figure is Shogaku no Shaka (the All-wise Buddha) represented in the act of preaching. Dispersed among the rockwork about him, are:—*The Rakan Batsudara* and his tiger. *The Bosatsu* (holy being) *Jizo*, protector of travelers and children, who carries upon his back an image of the child, Buddha, and in his right hand a *shakujo* (ringed staff).
>
> *Jizo's attendant*, carrying (by aid of a bearing pole) a lotus seat, for the image on Jizo's back, and a bell and sacred scrolls tied in a cloth.
>
> *The Rakan,* **Inkada** *Sonja*, seated in a meditative pose with his chin resting upon a Buddhist sceptre. His ordinary title, in **Japanese,** is *Inkatsu-da*. He is usually represented in the act of meditation.

The Rakan, Naga-saina. Dipping water from a fall. He is generally depicted as magically producing water from a bowl.

The attendant of the dragon Rishi burning incense in a *koro.*

The dragon Rishi, Chinnan, working magic by causing a dragon to ascend from his begging bowl.

A child amazed at the spiritual manifestation of the dragon Rishi.

Shussan no Shaka. Buddha returning from the mountain.

Vide " Legend of the Golden Lotus," pp. 7-10, in " The Golden Lotus," by Edward Greey.

All these figures were carved by the same artist.

Signed, "*Dai Nipon, Tokyo, Shima-mura Shun-mei.*"

Made by Shima-mura Shuns-mei, of Tokyo, Great Japan.

401.—Okimono (ornament), in the form of a Yebi (cray-fish). Ivory Carving. Made in Tokyo, Japan. H. 1½ in.; L. 16 in. Date, 1885.

The artist has treated the ivory so as to faithfully reproduce the appearance of the various parts of the *yebi,* even to the serrated edges of the feelers and the soft tissues of the under side of the body.

Made by *Nobu-toshi,* (signed).

402.—Netsuke (button) of tobacco pouch. Ivory Carving. Made in Tokyo, Japan. H. 1¼ in.; D. 3 in. Date, 1870-80.

On obverse a Chinese boy holding a white flower, some rocks and a stone upon which writing ink is ground. Boy has a writing-brush in his hand. *On reverse,* maker's name, *Ko-riu Sai,* and his seal. Also a scroll on which is written the following poem :

"I sometimes recline under a pine-tree
And sleep soundly,
With only a stone for my pillow."

(Not signed). Written by Ri-haku.

403.—**Netsuke** (button), **for an inro** (medicine-box), **in the form of a pine-cone. Ivory Carving.** Made in Tokyo, Japan. H. 1½ in.; D. 1 in. Date, 1850-80.

Outside decorated with a spray of pine. Screw, in form of a plum blossom. Cone opens into two sections, carved inside. Subject "The Old Couple of Takasago."
Signed, *Kwaigioku, Sai*.

404.—**Okimono** (ornament), **of deerhorn, vase-shaped. Japanese.** H. 2 in.; D. 2 in. Date, 1850-80.

Lid surmounted by Rakan reading from a scroll. Sides decorated with *Shishi* and *Botan*, in relief, in **ivory and** mother-of-pearl.

405.—**Vase. Iron, inlaid with gold. Chinese.** H. 6¼ in.; Base, 1½ in.; D. 2¼ in. Date, 1426-35. (*Seuen-te* period, Ming dynasty).

Round the edges, base and neck are bands of key pattern between these, floral scrolls and conventional peacocks. On the bottom *Ta Min Seuen-te nen sei*. (Great Ming Seuen-te period.)

"This vase is said to have been in the possession of the celebrated *virtuoso* Kobori Masakadzu. The date it bears is one that has been more largely forged than perhaps any other, except that of the *Wan-leih* period, *but the authenticity of this vase is beyond question*. Its picture and description appear in a MSS. entitled *Meihin-roku* (Catalogue of Precious Objects) which enjoys a wide reputation among Japanese dilettanti."—*Brinkley*.

(From the collection of Captain F. Brinkley, R. A. Tokyo, Japan.)

406.—**Incense-burner, in the form of a war-drum, upon which is perched a crowing cock. Japanese Silver.** Made in Tokyo. H. 13½ in.; D. 6 in. Date, 1880.

Signed, *Hagi-ya Katsu-hei.*

The body of the drum is overlaid with copper, simulating wood, over which is a running plant. The faces of the drum are decorated with applique figures of the *Howo*. The cock is composed of gold, silver, *shakudo* and *shibuichi*.

The harmonious blending of metals, the grace, spirit and action of the cock and the admirable contempt for the intrinsic compared with the æsthetic value of the materials used, show the careful study and artistic feeling of the metal-worker, and prove that the Japanese, even in these degenerate days, when well paid, and when permitted to exercise the knowledge transmitted by their ancestors and teachers, can produce works of the highest excellence.

407.—**Perfume-box (*Ko-bako*), Japanese, Gold, Silver and Shibuichi.** Made in Tokyo. H. 4½ in.; Square, 2¾ in. Date, 1880.

Four panels. Two decorated with archaic forms of birds, etc. The third in semi-relief, Dai-koku holding open his bag of riches for his familiars, the rats, to fill. The fourth, the rats are busily engaged in plundering a treasure-box of its golden *rio*, which they carry to their patron.

Signed, *Sei-jiu Rio-un Sai.* On the base is an inlaid seal: *Gaku Soku* (To Enjoy Rule).

(*No.* 571. *Morgan Collection.*)

408.—**Group of tortoises upon a rock. Japanese Bronze.** H. 7 in.; Base, 10½ in. Date, 1825.

Made by Seimin, who died in 1838.

Signed: "Cast by Seimin, whose artist name is Saigioku, when sixty-six years old, on eighteenth day of the fifth month of the 8th year (Bird year) period of Bunsei (June, 1825).

The Tortoise symbolizes long life, the rock, solidity. (H. S.)

409.—**Fuye** (flute). **Japanese Iron, inlaid with silver, brass, copper and shakudo.** In a copper and brass case. L. 16 in. Date, 1767.

The case bears an inscription, in raised characters, of which the following is a free translation:

"There are many iron flutes in China, but only a few in our country, (Japan,) so I tried to make one, and, after carefully hammering and tempering the metal, I finally succeeded.

"One day, a man (famous musician) who called upon me, played on this, then said 'This is a very good flute, its voice is tuneful.' I answered him, 'Although I am aware that my work is poor I shall be very happy if any one else (but such a virtuoso) is able to play on this flute.'

"I have inscribed this on the case of this *fuye* so that it will remain for ever and ever, and all men shall know of it.

"Fourth Year of the Period of Meiwa, first part of Summer (1767).

"Written by the maker, Senhoku" (Spring-north) or literally "Spring-north, making-man, also wrote this."

A relic of Old Japan. It, like its Chinese prototype, has evidently been modeled on the very ancient bamboo flute, bound with silk to keep it from splitting.

The decoration, a spiritual dragon, is of such pure silver that it does not oxidize. The clouds are of brass and the appendages of the dragon of *Shakudo* tipped with red copper. The end is stopped with a beautifully carved cherry blossom, in silver. It has been lined with red lacquer to prevent the formation of rust.

410.—**Yatate. Case for writing implements. Japanese Shibuichi.** Made for the sign of a *Yatate* seller in Asakusa, Tokyo. H. 3¾ in.; L. 17½ in. Date, 1868.

Exquisitely decorated with a spiritual dragon in semi-relief. Signed, "Made by Midzu-tani Ichi-sen, Yatate maker. Decorated by Sei min, whose artist name is To-un Sai, for the Yatate seller Otome Chuzo, who lives at Okura mage, Asakusa, Tokyo."

It contains a receptacle for black ink, and places for writing-brushes and an eraser. Also spaces for red ink, for seal and for writing. The ordinary *yatate* is about seven inches long and is carried in the sleeve or girdle.

411.—**Yatate. Case for writing implements. Japanese Copper.** H. 1½ in.; L. 8 in. Date, 1800-50.

Design, lotus stem and leaves. Bowl, seed-pod of lotus, surmounted by a frog. Stem is inscribed with the following poem:
> "While sleeping, a breeze enters my room.
> Making verses soothes me."

or,
> "Composing poetry soothes me
> Like the breeze that enters my room at night."

412.—**Yatate. Case for holding writing implements. Japanese Brass.** H. 1⅞ in.; L. 7 in. Date, 1800-50.

Square stem and bowl. Decoration, *Shishi* and Buddhistic designs, in relief. *Ojime* (slide), brass.

413.—**Incense-burner, in the form of a Crab. Japanese Bronze.** H. 3½ in.; L. 8½ in. Date, 15th century. (Probably older).

Very curious: not only on account of its archaic form, but also from the fact that, prior to the fifteenth century, objects like this were made of sheet-metal and not cast.

414.—**Image of Amida Buddha, standing upon an inverted lotus. Japanese Bronze.** H. 12½ in.; D. 5 in. Date, before the 14th century.

Has been heavily gilt. Inclosed in a quaint box, made of iron plates riveted together.

(Purchased by me in Nara, in 1882. Its owner stated that it was made during period of *Eiku*, 1113-1117. It is without doubt a very old specimen.—*E. G.*)

415.—Incense-burner, in the form of an *ascending Koi (carp,) **in two sections.** Japanese Bronze. Made in **Nagasaki.** L. 7 in. Date, early part of 18th century.

>Made by Kamejo (O'Kamé) of Nagasaki, said to have been the first Japanese woman to make bronze *okimono* (decorative objects). Her works are now very rare.
>Unsigned, but inscribed with the following poem:
>"Say not that the fish remains too long in the water,
>The time will come when it will rise."
>
> (H. S.)

416.—Tray of an Incense-box. Japanese Lacquer. H. ¼ in.; L. 3¾ x 3 in. Date, 1750-60.

>Decoration, scene on **Lake** Biwa, the details of which are very beautiful.

417.—Tea-jar. Japanese **Lacquer.** H. 3 in.; D. 3 in. Date, 1780-1800.

>*Nashiji* (pear-skin) lacquer. Top decorated with the Tokugawa *mon* (crest), three hollyhock leaves, conventionalized, in a circle.

418.—Incense-box, in the **form of a Fan. Japanese** Lacquer. H. 1 in.; D. 4 in. Date, 1830-50.

>Decoration, foliage, in gold and black.

419.—Incense-box, copper-lined. **Japanese Lacquer.** H. 2½ in.; D. 2½ in. Date, 1800-50.

>Curious imitation of wood. Lid decorated to resemble a basket.

---

*The ascending carp symbolizes ambition, vigor and perseverance.

420.—**Box, in the form of three clam-shells, overlapping. Japanese Lacquer.** H. 3½ in.; L. 7½ in. Date, 1650-1700.

>Lid, decoration, scene in Kamakura. Some of the pine-trees made of brilliant colored nacre overlaid with lines of lacquer. Body covered with a quaint diapering representing straw mats (such as are used to bale rice) on which are represented shells. Scratched on the lid, *Hime-kishi* (lady-shore)—probably the name of the scene.
>
>Curious lacquer, every detail of which, outside and in, is worth examining through a glass.

421.—**Tobacco-pouch, or Koshi-sage,** (box for everything). **Made** of shagreen **and fish-bones. Japanese.** H. 2¾ in.; D. 3¼ in. Date, 1800-50.

>Carved slide. Pipe-case, of deerhorn, to represent bamboo.

422.—**Tea-jar. Cinnibar Layer-Lacquer. Japanese.** H. 2¼ in.; D. 2¼ in. Date, 1700-1800.

>Made by applying repeated layers of cinnibar and other colored lacquer to the body of the object. After a final, heavy body of cinnibar was applied, the object was carved so as to show the different strata.

423.—**Netsuke, button of tobacco-pouch, in the form of a seated figure, performing the ceremony of Oniwa Soto. Japanese Wood-carving.** H. 2 in.; Base, 3 in. Date, 1850-80.

>*Oniwa Soto* (expelling demons) is a ceremony performed on the fifteenth day after the shortest day (December twenty-first), *i. e.*, on January fifth. The object being to expel evil spirits and attract the good to the house.

424.—**Tobacco-pouch of** leather, **with** gold ojime (slide) and black **wood** pipe-case, inlaid with **silver and other metals.** Japanese. Pouch, square, 4x3½ in.; pipe-case, 8¼ in. long. Date, 1850-1880.

>*Ojime* made by *Sei-ken-ko, Kan-ji.*

425.—**Figure of Shussan No Shaka.** (Buddha just before he attained Nirvana) **Japanese Wood-carving.** H. 9 in.; Base, 3x2 in. Date, about 1600.

> The ascetic face and worn form of the Buddha are beautifully rendered.

426.—**Writing-table** (*Bundai*) of *Jodai-mono Lacquer. **Japanese.** H. 4½ in.; Top, 22x12½ in. Date, 1145-50. (Period of *Ki-nan*).

> Decoration, landscape with pine trees and birds, copied from a Chinese painting. It was once the property of the great Shogun Yoritomo of the Minamoto clan, who ruled, for the Emperor, at Kamakura from 1185-99. From him it finally passed into the possession of the eighth Ashikaga Shogun, the renowned Yoshimasa, 1449-71, who presented it to Kwanji, a famous "No" dancer, to whom he also presented the *Sudsuri Bako* No. 427 of this collection.

427.—**Writing-Implement box,** (*sudsuri bako*). †**Jidai-mono Lacquer. Japanese.** H. 2 in.; Square, 9x8½ in. Date, 1288-93. (Period of *Sho-o*).

> Decoration, *chidori* (literally "snipe," but metaphorically "thousand birds"). Very curious, archaic style.
>
> This box was termed *Yamagaëura* on account of its beauty for, although dulled with age, it must have once been both brilliant and glossy.
>
> Both of these specimens of rare and valuable lacquer, (Nos. 426 and 427), were kept in the family of Kwanji and treasured as heirlooms by his descendants until after the revolution of 1871, when poverty compelled the possessors to part with them. In 1878 they were purchased, from the descendants of Kwanji, by an American gentleman who was in the service of the Japanese government, and were kept by him until December, 1886.

---

*Made before the reign of Emperor Gotoba, 1185-98.
†Made between 1186-1688.

www.ingramcontent.com/pod-product-compliance
Lightning Source LLC
Chambersburg PA
CBHW022131160426
43197CB00009B/1239